Secrets of the New Age

Secrets of the New Age

Discover the Sources
of the Supernatural Powers and
Prophetic Messages That
Are Sweeping Americans Into a
New Spiritual Allegiance

Kenneth R. Wade

REVIEW AND HERALD® PUBLISHING ASSOCIATION
WASHINGTON, DC 20039-0555
HAGERSTOWN, MD 21740

This book was
Edited by Richard W. Coffen
Designed by Bill Kirstein
Cover photo by Meylan Thoresen

Scripture quotations marked NASB are from the *New American Standard Bible*, © The Lockman Foundation 1960, 1962, 1963, 1968, 1971, 1972, 1973, 1975, 1977.

Texts credited to NIV are from the *Holy Bible, New International Version*. Copyright © 1973, 1978, International Bible Society. Used by permission of Zondervan Bible Publishers.

Bible texts credited to RSV are from the Revised Standard Version of the Bible, copyrighted 1946, 1952 © 1971, 1973.

R&H Cataloging Service

Wade, Kenneth Robert, 1951-
    Secrets of the new age.

    1. New age movement—Controversial literature.
I. Title.

133

ISBN 0-8280-0520-6

Contents

C H A P T E R
1

In Search of the New Age

Dr. Edgar D. Mitchell leaned against a brown Cadillac parked in an alley just off Constitution Avenue in Washington, D.C. Taking a long drag on his cigarette, he looked me over carefully, no doubt wondering just where my questions would lead. The green PRESS ribbon attached to my identification badge waved lightly in the cool November breeze. Together we had walked down the alley between two massive gray government buildings to catch a little midday sun.

Dr. Mitchell is founder and president of the Institute of Noetic Sciences, which because of its research in the area of human potential, is considered a part of the New Age movement. But that is not his original claim to fame. His name became a household word in 1971 when, as pilot of the Apollo 14 lunar module, Mitchell became the sixth man to set foot on the moon.

The institute was sponsoring a three-day "Greater Self" conference inside the General Services Administration building, just across the street from the Smithsonian Institution's National Museum of American History.

I had come here in pursuit of answers about the New Age movement. Answers to questions such as What sort of people are involved? Why is there so much fascination with Hinduism and other Eastern religions among people interested in the New Age? What part does channeling and contact with spirit entities play in the movement? Should Christians cooperate with it, or is the movement anti-Christian in nature?

But these were just preliminary questions. The more I learned about the New Age movement, the more fascinated I became—and the more questions I had. Also, the questions became significant for my understanding of biblical prophecy, the relationship between Christianity and New Age, and what we can expect to happen in the near future.

I found a lot of answers that day. But I left with more unanswered questions than I had arrived with. The New Age movement, it seems, is not easy to pin down or define. It is too broad and has no easily defined central organization or leadership. The Institute of Noetic Sciences is part of the movement, but whether it is at the core or the fringes depends on which branch of the movement defines it.

A good analogy to the diversity within the New Age movement is the denominations within Christianity. Just as Baptists and Episcopalians share certain core beliefs but differ on other doctrines, so groups who consider themselves part of the New Age movement may hold widely differing beliefs but share a few core ideas. And just as Baptists look to a different group of leaders than Episcopalians do, so those who believe in the New Age follow various leaders who have differing viewpoints and agendas. No well-defined "denominations" exist within the New Age movement yet, but given enough time and the operation of human nature, no doubt many will soon appear.

The breadth of the movement makes it all the more interesting. And all the more important that we understand it.

New Age Books

From Constitution Avenue my search for understanding led me down Pennsylvania Avenue, past the Capitol building, to the Library of Congress. There I used the computer facilities to prepare a list of every book in English cataloged since 1968 that had the words *New Age* in the title—310 titles in all. Then I did a subject search and printed out another list of books that were included under that subject heading.

Days of research in the reading rooms of the greatest library in the world yielded some answers and pointed me toward new areas that needed investigation—particularly when I discovered books with such titles as *Occult Preparations for a New Age*, *Pagan Occult New Age Directory*, and *UFOs: Key to the New Age*.

Next I stopped at Georgetown, on the other end of downtown Washington. There a New Age bookstore beckoned. By this time I had pretty well concluded that I would never be able to pin down exactly what the New Age movement stands for. And a couple hours of browsing the bookshelves there confirmed my opinion. The well-organized shop had sections devoted to primitive religions, African philosophies, reincarnation and karma, transcendentalism, tantra, and dozens of other topics. Still, my research there did provide some important clues as to the real roots of the movement.

Soon I discovered that used-book stores could provide important clues to the origin of the concept that our world is headed for drastic changes that will shortly (before the year 2000, in fact, according to most writers) usher in the New Age of enlightenment and increased harmony. Used-book stores were an important resource because their metaphysics and occult sections often had out-of-print paperback books that I couldn't find in libraries. I was astounded when I discovered the number of books that had been written in the late 1960s and early 1970s by people who at that time claimed to be receiving messages about the coming New Age.

But even more important was the origin of the messages. The people receiving the messages claimed to be hearing from sources such as UFOs, extraterrestrials, Ouija boards, spirit guides, and spirits of long-dead leaders who had passed on to higher planes of existence.

God on the Moon

But to get back to my visit with Dr. Mitchell, the two of us stood in that sunny alley for 40 minutes while I plied him with questions. I wanted to reach the roots of the New Age movement.

My interest in the former astronaut's ideas stemmed from something I had read in a book he edited in 1974. Describing his experience on the moon, he wrote, "The first thing that came to mind as I looked at Earth was its incredible beauty. Even the spectacular photographs do not do it justice. It was a majestic sight—a splendid blue and white jewel suspended against a velvet black sky. . . . In a peak experience, the presence of divinity became almost palpable, and I *knew* that life in the universe was not just an accident based on random processes" (in John White, ed., *Psychic Exploration*, p. 29).

That excited me. Especially when I learned that Mitchell is regarded as a leader in the New Age movement. If he was serious about encountering divinity on the moon, perhaps this was an indication that the movement is based on a search for contact with God.

I asked Dr. Mitchell about his experience of divinity, particularly about the tie-in that I had noticed between the New Age movement and a historic movement called spiritualism. The conference had included a presentation on channeling that, in some of its manifestations, seemed to me to be just a modern way of describing spirit mediumship. I wanted to know how a man who had experienced God's presence on the moon could feel comfortable contacting spirits that I had always thought of as fallen angels. From my study of Scripture their mission is not to bring about a New Age of harmony, but to deceive people and lead the world to the great battle of Armageddon.

As I probed Dr. Mitchell's thinking, I soon became convinced that here was a man who, despite what he had said about sensing the presence of divinity on the moon, did not actually believe in God at all. At least not God as I had come to understand Him through the years.

I learned that he regarded contacts with supernatural spirits from a purely rationalistic viewpoint. In his view the powers that channels, mediums, and primitive shamans, or witch doctors, contact are not really supernatural beings at all. Rather the individuals who make these contacts are specially gifted people who can tap in to something called the "morphogenetic field"—a field of knowledge similar to what psychiatrist Carl Jung called the "collective unconscious." It is a body of knowledge almost like instinct and is common to and available to anyone who learns to make contact with it.

Two other contacts I made that day also helped me begin to understand the New Age movement better.

Shifting Paradigms

While sitting in the press lounge, I spoke with a distinguished-looking sixtyish gentleman. He identified himself as the husband of a woman who was to make a presentation at the conference. In the course of conversation, I learned that he had a Christian background, so I asked him one of the questions that most puzzled me about the New Age movement. "Why do you think that the movement's supporters lean so strongly toward Eastern rather than Western forms of religious experience?"

He replied that he had given considerable thought to the question. After briefly reviewing the history of religion and change in society, he postulated that our society is undergoing a significant transition of systems of belief—a *transformation*, or *paradigm shift*. Religion tends to favor maintaining the status quo and to resist transition and change. He pointed out that in the nineteenth century, Christian missionaries had set out to convert the world to Christianity, but that in the process they had spread Western culture more effectively than they had spread their religion.

"In those cultures that missionaries most influenced," he said, "the Christian perspective had played an important role in bringing about change. Even though they may not have succeeded in converting the people to Christianity, the missionaries did change the way the people viewed the world. They helped primitive peoples break loose from the traditions, taboos, and superstitions that had preserved their culture. This change of religious perspective worked a transformation of culture.

"So," he proposed, "the chief reason those who seek to bring a change for the better in our society look eastward for their philosophical framework is that they find the Christian institutions of the West too hidebound by tradition to support the kinds of changes bringing in the New Age requires."

I found his theory intriguing. But further research convinced me that it was a bit naive.

In observing the crowd of approximately 1,000 people at the conference, and in talking to a number of participants, I discovered that New Age thinking appeals to a wide spectrum of people. I had thought that I might find only starry-eyed ex-hippies, or perhaps young, naive students there. But I found businesspeople, retirees, young professionals, and thinking people from all classes and age groups.

They all seemed to have a positive concern for improving our world. A young mother I spoke with said, "I like to attend conferences like this because they are a welcome break from the high-pressured business world I have to deal with daily."

Though some of the people I spoke with had a strong Christian or Jewish background, none seemed to have given much thought to whether New Age ideas harmonized with their religion.

The Yogi Look

But Dr. Daniel Brown, a professor from Harvard University who made a presentation entitled " 'Inner

Science' Secrets of Tibetan Yogis," clearly did understand the relationship between Christian or Western meditation and the Eastern meditation techniques that form an important part of the New Age movement.

I interviewed Dr. Brown and learned that his research in altered states of consciousness (such as those achieved through hypnosis and certain types of meditation practiced in Eastern religions) has led him to spend much of his life studying Eastern religions, especially Buddhism. In the course of his studies he traveled to Tibet and studied under some of the meditation masters there.

"Why Tibet?" I asked. "Why the fascination with Eastern meditation as opposed to Western?"

He answered by describing the long background of Tibetan meditation. For more than a millennium prior to the Chinese conquest during the 1950s, entire families devoted themselves to nothing but meditation, and they identified many different levels of consciousness. "They have," he said, "probed into areas of the mind that we Westerners never even realized existed." So he believes that we can learn much about the mind from the Tibetans.

I asked Dr. Brown about the differences between Eastern and Western meditation. I had heard that the Eastern variety focused inward (toward nothing), whereas the Western kind focused outward (in search of God).

At first he seemed reluctant to agree with this perception, but the more I probed, the more he concurred. In the end he agreed that the direction one goes in meditation and in one's search for understanding depends upon whether or not one believes there is a god out there somewhere to contact. Meditation in the Tibetan, or Buddhist, vein works from the assumption that there is no personal God to be contacted, so it looks inward for answers. On the other hand, Christian meditation starts from the assumption that there is a personal God with whom we can and should communicate.

Other interviews at that conference also proved enlightening. But those three were like seeds planted in my mind. Oh, they did not bear fruit immediately. But as I continued to plow and harrow the soil of the New Age movement, the seeds that had been planted there sprouted and provided a rich crop of understanding.

But it was not until I came to understand the jargon—what Dr. Mitchell meant by terms such as *divinity* and *peak experience*—that I really understood how a man could claim to have contacted divinity and still remain, for all practical purposes, an atheist. It had puzzled me how someone could know ''that life in the universe was not just an accident based on random processes'' yet be a thoroughgoing evolutionist.

The insight I needed dawned upon me as I came to better understand the history of the New Age movement and the background of the New Age understanding of and agenda for life on earth.

CHAPTER
2

Roots of the New Age Movement

At first I thought the New Age movement was something that developed in the late 1970s. I didn't become aware of it until the middle 1980s. A 1987 *Time* magazine cover story titled "New Age Harmonies" reported that "nobody seems to know exactly where the term [New Age] came from, but it has been around for several decades or more" (*Time*, Dec. 7, p. 62).

But the New Age movement did not begin in the 1970s. In fact, it is just the latest expression of a movement that has been active in various ways for thousands of years. In its present form it is a network of organizations with similar interests, but with no central organization or hierarchical structure.

In 1980 *The Aquarian Conspiracy*, by Marilyn Ferguson, a leading New Age writer and proponent, was published. It is still probably the most important book ever written about the movement. Ferguson called the New Age movement an "Aquarian Conspiracy" and described it as "a leaderless but powerful network" that was "working to bring about radical change in the United States" (p. 23). She implied that the movement had been gaining support for many years.

My research at the Library of Congress turned up books with a New Age theme written in the mid-1960s. And the books I found in stores confirmed that New Age ideas had begun appearing in the popular press around 1965, although hope for a New Age had been prevalent among various cults and occult groups long before that.

The idea that we need something new to fix the ills of our world is certainly not revolutionary. Some called the years after World War I the New Era. Several nineteenth-century journals published in New England had "New Age" in their titles. One book about the American Revolution was titled *A New Age Now Dawns*. And various commentators on the Gospels have implied that Jesus' purpose 2,000 years ago was to bring in a new age.

However, the New Age movement, as we see it manifested today, *is* in some ways new. It is radical, as Ferguson said, because "its members have broken with certain key elements of Western thought, and they may even have broken continuity with history" (*ibid.*).

This element of a break with Western thought was what I explored in my interview with Dr. Brown. It is an essential key to understanding the significance of the movement.

The real philosophical underpinning of the New Age movement lies in this break with the West and the longing look to Eastern religious concepts for solutions to human needs. Probably a large number of people with New Age leanings are not at all familiar with the Theosophical Society. Yet many of the foundational concepts of the movement are based on that society's literature and on the writings of Alice Bailey, who left the society to found the Lucifer Trust (now called the Lucis Trust). The Theosophical Society's founders later moved from England to India and claimed to have received special letters containing hidden wisdom from Tibet.

When Alice Bailey broke with the society, she did not lose contact with the Tibetan sources. She claimed that she received her information, including instructions for bringing in the New Age, from Tibet via telepathy from a teacher called Djwhal Khul, whom she never met face-to-face. Bailey died in 1949, and now Benjamin Creme receives messages from Djwhal Khul. Creme is head of an organization that sponsored full-page newspaper advertisements proclaiming "The Christ Is Now Here" in 1982.

Apart from these mystical sources of Tibetan inspiration, several New Age thought leaders have studied under Tibetan masters. And Tibet's top holy man, Bstan-'dzin-rgya-mtsho, known also as the Dalai Lama, now addresses large audiences of New Age-oriented people around the world.

Thus a modified form of Tibetan Buddhism provides much of the underpinning of New Age thought. So it is important to understand something about Buddhism to really understand the movement.

The Enlightenment of Siddhartha

Buddhism's founder, Siddhartha Gautama, later known as the Buddha, began life as a Hindu prince. However, he found no satisfaction in Hinduism's answers to his questions about why so much suffering scourges the world. After six years of life as an ascetic, living for long periods eating only a grain of rice a day,

Siddhartha perceived that asceticism was not the key to enlightenment. Finally he sat down under a sacred fig tree to meditate until he could understand the reason for suffering.

While he sat there, various demons tempted him with answers, but he rejected all their suggestions. Finally, after more than 40 days of meditation, he entered a new state of being, between consciousness and unconsciousness. In that state he received the great enlightenment that earned him the name Buddha, which means "enlightened one."

The substance of his enlightenment is known as the Four Great Truths of Buddhism. But at one point Buddha himself condensed his wisdom into two points: (1) life is chiefly composed of suffering, and (2) it is possible to escape from suffering (Nancy Wilson Ross, *Three Ways of Asian Wisdom*, p. 81). His way of escape is through entrance into a state called *nirvana*, in which a person is no longer aware of any bodily needs or desires and in which reincarnation into another body with needs and desires is no longer necessary.

Translated literally, nirvana means "a blowing out"—as in blowing out the flame of a candle. Buddhists view life as a flickering flame that goes on and on in repeated manifestations until the person becomes enlightened enough to achieve nirvana. Buddha explained that each successive life a person lives is like the different flames that might be lit on the wick of a lamp from night to night. Although the oil remains the same in the reservoir, each night the flame is different. The oil represents the life, which has various manifestations in various lifetimes, or flames.

When one achieves nirvana, his lamp can be blown out and need never be lit again. Since, to Buddha, all life is suffering, the achievement of a state in which life no longer has to be lived is the goal to be most sought after.

New Age teachers typically popularize reincarnation by replacing the idea that all life is suffering with the more appealing idea that each life is a learning, growing experience. And instead of teaching that the ultimate goal is a blowing out, they suggest either that spirits go on living and improving for eternity or that life's goal is, as the Hindus believe, to become united with Brahman—the nonpersonal oneness of the whole universe.

The New Age Dogma

Belief in reincarnation (or transmigration as it is called in Hinduism) is the most basic tenet of New Age teaching. But one of the reasons that it is difficult to pin down exactly what the movement stands for is that the teachings derived from this basic tenet vary widely among the groups that identify themselves as New Age. It is safe to say, however, that virtually all New Age teachers add a second tenet to reincarnation—a belief in the evolution of spirits.

The theory of spiritual evolution is different from, but related to, the theory of evolution you may have studied in biology class. It does not emphasize evolution of life from one species to another. Rather, it teaches that individual immortal spirits go through multiple lifetimes on various levels, or planes, of existence. Life as a human being is only one of these planes. From this life a person's spirit may go on to live on another plane—perhaps on another planet or in a totally different form, without a physical body.

These two tenets form the foundation of the one major dogma that a person must accept in order to be a bona fide part of the current New Age movement: Earth and the beings on it are currently undergoing a time of crisis because we have arrived at a point in the evolution of the human spirit at which we are breaking over into a higher, more perfected realm of existence. This higher realm is the New Age. Some groups teach that it has already arrived, whereas others anticipate its inception in the near future. Belief in the presence or imminence of the New Age is, at its deepest core, what the New Age movement is all about.

The Spirit Connection

The ways in which this basic core dogma of hope is expressed are many, varied, confusing, and some-times confused. Perhaps this is because much of the basis for belief in the New Age comes from the teachings of various spirit beings who claim to be speaking from different planes. And the spirit commu-nicators give different messages to different groups.

Few if any New Age thinkers base their hopes for the New Age purely on rational thought to the exclu-sion of revelations from the spirit world. Even those who don't think the messages come from spirits living elsewhere still accept the messages as coming from the morphogenetic field or some such. (In chapters 4 and 5, I'll deal extensively with the New Age messages that are coming through various channels.)

It is important to realize that the basic tenets which open the way for belief in the dogma of expectation derive from Buddhist and Hindu teachings.

Inward Journey or Outward Search

Though the goals of Hinduism and Buddhism are seemingly opposite—they start from opposite assump-tions (Hinduism assumes the existence of a god with whom we can unite; Buddhism assumes that there is no god)—the method of achieving the goal is basically the same. It could be called the "inward journey," which looks for solutions through the discovery of insights that already dwell within the human mind. For this reason, Eastern religion and the New Age movement appeal to anyone who prefers belief in the great potential of human beings unaided by deity —hence to anyone who does not sense the need of a god or savior.

Christianity, Judaism, and the Muslim religions, on the other hand, trace their roots to Abraham, whose story the Bible relates in Genesis 11-25.

Abraham discovered God amidst his attempts to make a go of life unaided. He was a wise and successful businessman who knew just how to turn a profit *without* any divine intervention.

But it is also the story of a God who takes a personal interest in human beings and who intervened in Abraham's life to help him—despite Abraham's attempts to do everything on his own. It is the story of a God who wants very badly to interact in a positive way with people. Abraham's God wants people to respond positively to Him with trust, friendship, and obedience. And so Abraham discovered that it is good to have God for a friend.

Thus Western religion is founded on the belief (1) that there is a God outside of us, (2) that He can be contacted, and (3) that He wants to help us.

The New Age movement is founded on the premise that the Eastern inward look and Western outward focus are really the same thing at their core and that the two can somehow be melded together.

The problem is that the two belief systems start from opposite assumptions and (predictably) arrive at opposite conclusions. So in any effective melding one has to dominate and largely exclude the other. A traffic signal that shines red and green simultaneously is worthless.

So what the New Age movement ends up being is not an equal blending of East and West, as it claims. Either East or West has to dominate.

Findhorn

At the core of the current New Age movement is a community called Findhorn. Many if not most of the movement's leaders have visited or lived at Findhorn. The development of Findhorn illustrates what typically happens when people try to meld Eastern and Western religions.

The roots of the community go back to 1953 when Peter and Eileen Caddy visited Glastonbury, England. In her book *The Findhorn Garden* Eileen Caddy describes Glastonbury as "a center of spiritual power" (p. 36). Exactly what she means by that phrase is unclear, but in *Passages About Earth* William Irwin Thompson, a prominent New Age leader, tells of visiting Findhorn and being taken by Peter Caddy to "the power point of Cluny Hill." Peter explained to him that Cluny was "one of the points that Jesus had visited with His uncle, Joseph of Arimathea, and that they had come there from that other cosmic power point, Glastonbury" (p. 181).

I am not certain about the origin of the power point concept or of the legend of Joseph of Arimathea's having visited the British Isles with Jesus, but the ideas clearly have a Gnostic or mystical background. The Bible never calls Joseph Jesus' uncle and certainly never mentions a trip to Britain.

While meditating at Glastonbury, Eileen heard a voice speaking to her from within her mind. At first the voice said simply, "Be still, and know that I am God" (a quotation from the Bible), but later went on to explain that human beings—indeed, everything in the world—are a part of God (see Findhorn Community, pp. 36, 37). So the Caddys started from a Western mystical background and soon progressed to Eastern pantheism.

During the ensuing years the Caddys came to know the voice that spoke to Eileen as "the God within." This god asked her, "Do you not realize that you have within you all wisdom, all knowledge, all understanding? You do not have to seek it without, but you have to take time to be still and to go deep within to find it" (*ibid.*).

This sort of teaching, of course, led the Caddys away from Western religion, away from Abraham's God, and into Eastern inward-focused religion.

Even so, Peter testified that by 1962 "we had learned to surrender everything, including our wills, to God."

In their spiritual quest to know the will of God, Peter and Eileen linked up with Dorothy Maclean, who had developed a facility for communicating with various spirit beings.

The Caddys and Ms. Maclean were employed from 1957 until 1962 at the Cluny Hill resort hotel in northern Scotland. Peter served as the hotel's manager. During his tenure there, the hotel prospered under the guidance that Dorothy received from the spirits.

Then at the end of the summer of 1962 the Caddys and Dorothy suddenly found themselves unemployed. But because they had learned to trust the god they knew, this did not worry them particularly. They simply took their small travel trailer and moved, along with the Caddys' three young sons, into a trailer park on nearby Findhorn Bay. (At some earlier time they had visited this park on holiday, and their spirit guides revealed to them that they would soon be returning there. Now upon their return they received the message that they were to stay there for some extended period of time.)

Carrots and Devas

As Peter tells the story in *The Findhorn Garden*, the six of them were compelled to live on unemployment benefits of about $80 per week. Despite his record of success at Cluny Hill, he was unable to find employment that winter. So Peter spent the short days and long evenings reading books on organic gardening.

The soil at Findhorn was more suitable for a quarry than for gardening. Tenacious clumps of grass and brambles had managed to collect just enough topsoil to eke out an existence, but digging revealed that an inch or so down the soil gave way to sand, and below that was gravel. The entire area seemed incapable of supporting any type of garden crop.

Yet the following spring, with the right mix of compost, organic fertilizer, backbreaking work, *and* communication with beings they called devas, the Caddys and Dorothy managed to raise several crops successfully.

In the following years they continued to expand their garden until it received local, then nationwide, attention. During this time they became convinced that the New Age would begin at the end of 1967 (Thompson, p. 158).

Before long, Sir George Trevelyan, who was the chief mover in the development both of adult education and of the New Age movement in England, paid a visit and left singing the praises of the Caddys and their spirit guides.

Today Findhorn enjoys worldwide fame. A small community thrives there, operating large gardens and a school to which people can come to study the principles that made Findhorn successful.

Those principles include not only the right methods of composting and the right use of cow manure, but also the right way to communicate with the spirits, gnomes, and fairies that inhabit the plants you want to grow.

Maybe you remember when talking to plants was popular. Well, the Findhorn community goes far beyond that. They not only talk—they listen. Here is part of Dorothy Maclean's testimony about her own experience with contacting the devas: "I used to do regular rounds with the liquid manure, asking each vegetable deva whether or not the plants would like a dose that day. Sometimes the response was just a direct Yes or No, while at other times it was combined with a bit of general information. . . . The carrot deva told us, 'The carrots are coming along nicely and could be missed when you put on another dose of liquid manure. You wonder why they are all right when the parsnips next to them are hungry. The carrots, through their special carrot quality, are able to convert energy from the radiations which parsnips do not tune into' " (Caddy, p. 62).

Peter Caddy explains that devas are "part of the angelic hierarchy that holds the archetypal pattern for each plant species and directs energy toward bringing a plant into form on the physical plane" (*ibid.*, p. 7).

About two months after starting the Findhorn garden, Dorothy Maclean first made contact with the deva of the garden pea through inward-focused meditation. The Findhorn family at first did not know what to call the beings. They finally chose the term *deva* rather than *angel* to describe them because *angel* is too closely tied to Western forms of religion, and Dorothy and the Caddys were much more interested in Eastern religion. *Deva* is a Sanskrit word meaning "divine, or shining one."

Among the New Age-oriented people who were soon attracted to Findhorn were R. Ogilvie Crombie and David Spangler. Crombie helped the community by introducing them to the gnomes that he claimed inhabited the various wild and cultivated flowers in their area. But it was not only gnomes that revealed themselves to Crombie, he even tells of having met and talked with the ancient pagan god Pan on the foggy, lamplit streets of Edinburgh.

In 1970 David Spangler and his soulmate, Myrtle Glines, stopped by for a visit and stayed for three years. While there, Spangler began to receive messages from a spirit that identified itself as Limitless Love and Truth (LL&T). This spirit's messages are recorded in Spangler's book *Revelation: The Birth of a New Age*. LL&T had earlier sent messages to other people in England, and these formed the basis for their belief that the New Age began at the end of 1967 (p. 63; see also Thompson, p. 158; Anthony Brooke, *Revelation for the New Age*, pp. 62, 64, 68, 79).

For years Spangler had communicated with various spiritual beings or powers. In *Revelation* he describes his first contact with one particular power.

"Not long after we [he and Myrtle] had begun working together, we were sitting in the living room of a friend when I felt like a strong presence had walked into the room. We were alone on a physical level, but I knew someone had entered. On impulse, I reached over and held Myrtle's hand. Almost immediately, I felt my identity being pulled away from its focus on myself and into communion with this presence. While remaining fully conscious and aware, I was immersed in a process of exchanging energy with this being and entering into its consciousness. As this happened, I felt a flow of impressions and words which I wished to share with Myrtle. It was as if my body was now the focus for an identity that was the joint creation of Myrtle's energy, my own, and that of this being. Eyes closed to maintain my inward concentration, I began to talk as if I were that identity, thus expressing outwardly at least that function and appearance of being a channel" (p. 48).

Thus Findhorn, and much of the New Age hope with it, is founded on a combination of Hinduism, Buddhism, and contacts with spirit entities, with a small measure of Christian mysticism thrown in to make it seem that the two sides of religion are given equal consideration.

And Findhorn is not an isolated phenomenon. All around the world similar communities have sprung up during the past two decades. And the belief systems typified there have become popular among millions of people in America and around the world.

The paradigm shift from Western to Eastern has already taken place for these people.

How has it happened so rapidly? Or has it been a gradual shift? And is the shift continuing? To that question we will turn in the next chapter.

CHAPTER
3

Preparations for the Movement

The book that everyone simply had to read in the early 1970s was *Jonathan Livingston Seagull*. First published in 1970, the book did not really catch on until 1972. But that year 1.8 million hardcover copies sold. It was the number one best-seller in both 1972 and 1973, and by 1975 more than 9 million copies were circulating (Alice Payne Hackett and James Henry Burke, *80 Years of Best-sellers*, pp. 10, 214). In it Richard Bach, who today is known as a leading New Age proponent, weaves an intriguing tale about a seagull who aspires to something higher in life than chasing fishing boats and squawking and fighting for crumbs and fishheads. Bach claims that a bird materialized and dictated the book to him (Brooks Alexander, "Theology From the Twilight Zone," *Christianity Today*, Sept. 18, 1987, p. 26).

Like his namesake David Livingstone, the nineteenth-century missionary who forsook the common ways of life and gave himself to a higher ideal, Jon the seagull forsakes the flock and strives to perfect the art of flying—to become a sort of superbird.

To a certain extent he succeeds, learning to fly faster and with more precision than any other gull in the flock. But the elders do not approve of his aerobatics, and soon he is banished to the Far Cliffs to live out his life in solitude.

While there he further perfects his flying, then in an episode reminiscent of the song "Swing Low, Sweet Chariot," he encounters two other gulls who can fly as well as he. They take him from the Far Cliffs to a higher realm of existence, which he at first thinks is heaven. Later he learns that this is just a higher level of being that gulls go to after they achieve enlightenment on the earthly plane. Most gulls, a friend tells him, have to go through 10,000 or more reincarnations before they reach this level.

In this new realm Jon studies under Chiang (the gull equivalent of an Eastern guru), who has learned to travel on the astral plane—that is, he can travel instantly from place to place simply by thinking himself to his destination. This seems to Jon as though it would be the ultimate superbird accomplishment. But he has trouble attaining it, until one day the light breaks through, and he realizes that he in and of himself, is a perfect, unlimited gull! Instantly he and Chiang find themselves on another planet.

But, Chiang says, this is not the ultimate trip. The next level is to learn to travel through time, and the final level is to "fly up and know the meaning of kindness and love" (Richard Bach, *Jonathan Livingston Seagull*, p. 60).

The rest of the story relates Jon's experiences in learning to love enough to go back and teach the very gulls who banished him. In the process he helps a favorite student discover that death is not death, but is merely a doorway to a new existence—to reincarnation.

Judging the impact of a book that sold so many copies is impossible. However, its images are powerful enough that, having read it for the first time just recently, I cannot see a gull flying without having the book's message forcefully called to mind.

Changing Viewpoints

How much credit Richard Bach deserves for fostering the changed viewpoints of Americans and others cannot be determined. But a 1982 Gallup poll revealed that 23 percent of Americans believed in reincarnation (Norman L. Geisler and J. Yutaka Amano, *The Reincarnation Sensation*, p. 7).

Bach's influence was just one among many forces that led to a change of paradigms for Americans and other Westerners.

A paradigm is a way of looking at things—the basic overall assumptions that one makes when deciding how or what to think about something. A shift of viewpoints takes time. Many New Age thinkers perceive that the paradigm shift we are witnessing in the world around us today is as deep as any since the Renaissance or even before. Writing from an evolutionist's viewpoint, Theodore Roszak, a leading historian of modern culture, compares the current transition to what happened when human beings first learned to speak.

It is a shift from traditional ways of thinking based on the Christian concept of a personal, caring God to belief that human beings are their own god. It is a shift from belief in death, judgment, and resurrection to belief in reincarnation; from belief in heaven and hell to belief that we create our own heaven or hell right here on earth; from belief in the grace of God for sinners to belief that every individual must pay for his or her wrongs in repeated lives of suffering; from belief that there is a God in control of our destiny to belief that we must, through planned evolution, improve our own lot.

The shift began a long time ago, but accelerated rapidly during the 1960s.

Spiritualistic Roots

Some of the roots for this change in paradigm go back to the beginning of modern spiritualism in Hydesville, New York, in 1848. Spiritualists claim to have the ability to communicate with the spirits of the deceased. Astrologer Dane Rudhyar, writing about the New Age in a book published by the Theosophical Society in 1975, sees great significance in the fact that the first knockings heard by the Fox sisters preceded by exactly 100 years the 1948 "arrival" of UFOs, which allegedly proclaim the coming of the New Age (*Occult Preparations for a New Age*, p. 43). More about that later!

Other roots go back to 1844 when the Persian prophet the Bab declared that the Islamic era had come to an end. In 1863 the Persian Baha'u'llah followed up on this by proclaiming himself the lawgiver for a New Age society (*ibid.*, pp. 10, 52). The Bahá'í faith, which is founded on his teachings, is still active today.

Despite spiritualism's surge in popularity during the middle of the nineteenth century and again during World War I, when many of the bereaved wanted to contact deceased relatives, these influences had little impact on the overall viewpoint in America and Europe.

As long as the majority of the people held the Bible in high esteem, the belief in reincarnation and the evolution of spirits would never gain wide acceptance. The paradigm shift had to wait.

Ready for a Shift

By the end of the first half of the twentieth century many people were abandoning their spiritual roots. They had been through two world wars and were largely disillusioned with Christianity because it had not brought in the millennium of peace that pre-World War I preachers had promised.

The accomplishments of modern technology and medicine added to people's complacency about things spiritual. The miraculous and supernatural were consigned, even by the outwardly religious, to the past. They were considered to be based on myths for which an enlightened age had outgrown its need.

This was also the age of the coming of the new morality and new sexual freedoms. Advances in infection control freed people from the fear of sexually transmitted diseases, and advances in birth control freed them from worry about conception. Cut loose from these two restraints, men and women abandoned the ancient mores and set out upon a sexual orgy that only the coming of AIDS has dampened.

The type of freedom that the sexual revolution gave to people is heady stuff—and not easy to leave behind. People enjoyed their freedom, and turned away from any religion that would restrict what they wanted to do.

But abandoning or ignoring the faith of their fathers did not erase the need for spirituality among Americans. It simply left them anchorless, spiritually adrift, waiting for a new wind.

It soon began to blow.

The Psychic Wind

If you're old enough to remember November 22, 1963, you probably remember where you were and what you were doing when you first heard that President John F. Kennedy had been shot.

You may also remember some of the interesting discussions that followed that event. A young psychic by the name of Jeanne Dixon had recently been attracting national attention. Her supposed ability to foresee coming events was well enough known that people widely asked, "If this lady could, indeed, predict the future, why didn't she warn Kennedy?" Dixon answered this question by saying that she had sensed something ominous, but had been unable to contact the president. Her answer satisfied enough people to redeem her reputation. Two years later a book about her life revealed that her premonition about the demise of the president elected in 1960 went clear back to 1952 (Ruth Montgomery, *A Gift of Prophecy*, pp. 1-6).

Other events from the same era piqued people's interest in the supernatural. Arthur Ford, another well-known psychic, conducted a seance in a television studio in Canada with Episcopal bishop James A. Pike present. Pike's son had committed suicide a year and a half earlier, and now Ford's "spirit guide" relayed messages purporting to be from the son and other deceased friends of the bishop. Pike testified that the messages contained intimate details that only the individuals claiming to speak from "the other side" could have known. Major Canadian and U.S. networks televised the program in 1967.

Meanwhile, the youth counterculture came to full flower. Led by men like Timothy Leary and Allen Ginsberg, teenagers whose main acquaintance with spiritual things consisted of memorizing portions of an ancient catechism—if they had had that much religious training—went on a wild search for any sort of spirituality that might present itself. Many people even proclaimed the spiritual implications of the widespread experimentation with LSD and other psychedelic drugs.

The youth counterculture's rebellion against the establishment included, but was by no means limited to, protests against the Vietnam War. In addition to their protesting, many of these same young people had embarked on an urgent search for a meaningful experience of spiritual power. Historian Theodore Roszak describes one antiwar rally at the Pentagon during which protesters resorted to occult incantations and spell-casting "in hopes of levitating that grim ziggurat right off the ground" (*The Making of a Counter Culture*, p. 124). Among the youths gathered that day were witches, warlocks, holy men, seers, prophets, mystics, saints, sorcerers, and shamans, according to a popular counterculture paper *The East Village Other* (*ibid.*).

Looking East

About this time Harvard University professor Richard Alpert, who had been associated with Timothy Leary in promoting use of LSD for the spiritual journey, became disillusioned with drugs. So he trekked to India and sought enlightenment at the feet of a Hindu guru named Neem Kanli Baba. The guru renamed Richard Alpert "Ram Dass." Describing the watershed decade in which all this happened, Dass wrote in 1976: "In the sixties the word God was still taboo, so we talked about 'altered states of consciousness.' "

"Most of us didn't bargain for the implications of

the trip we found ourselves on. We started to understand that it might have something to do with what had been talked about as 'God' or a 'coming to God' or, if you would rather deal with the unmanifest, the state of Nirvana" (Ram Dass, *Grist for the Mill*, p. 19).

Dass and other counterculture leaders popularized the idea of looking within for spiritual enlightenment, and the concept of "the God within" quickly took root among those who had never known the God who reveals Himself in the Bible.

Alan Watts was another popular speaker in those days. He did much to popularize Zen Buddhism, with its inward-focused meditation. In *Psychotherapy East and West*, published in 1961, he described the similarity between Eastern mysticism and psychotherapy, which at that time was becoming a popular substitute for spirituality.

Another popular therapeutic application of Eastern ideas came from Indian guru Maharishi Mahesh Yogi, who introduced transcendental meditation (TM) to the United States in 1959. Soon hundreds of thousands of people were using TM to relax, to allay tension, and even to reduce blood pressure.

Proponents of TM claimed that the technique could be beneficial without having any religious connotations whatever. Independent observers, however, pointed out that the word (called a *mantra*) given to meditators to repeat as they induced the meditative trance-state was always a "primal word" from the ancient scriptures. In chapter 9 I will deal more extensively with the effects of TM.

Further influence with a somewhat Eastern flavor came from Pierre Teilhard de Chardin, a Jesuit missionary to China who was forbidden by church authorities to publish his writings because of their evolutionary viewpoint. After his death in 1955, friends immediately rushed his manuscripts into print, and their popularity has continued to grow. In 1980 Marilyn Ferguson reported that a survey she had conducted revealed that De Chardin's writings had had a more profound influence on those she called "Aquarian conspirators" than the works of any other author (Ferguson, *The Aquarian Conspiracy*, p. 50).

Teilhard de Chardin's ideas contribute much to the basis of the evolutionary/reincarnationist philosophy that is so important to New Age thought. In 1934 he wrote a short book titled (in English) *How I Believe*. In it he argued that the immortal spirit has evolved to become human and thus is able to perceive. This evolution must continue until human consciousness becomes one with the universe. But this will be accomplished through ultimate differentiation, not through absorption into Brahman (p. 82). In this way he sought to meld Eastern pantheism with Christianity.

The Video Vision

The late sixties also saw the brief run of what has turned out to be one of the most influential television series ever aired. *Star Trek* was produced for only three seasons. But its popularity has multiplied since, and you can watch reruns in virtually every viewing market in the United States and in many areas of the world. To date, four movies spawned by the series have played to mammoth theater audiences, and in the late 1980s a program called *Star Trek, the Next Generation* was being broadcast. Many "Trekkies," as the show's compulsive fans are called, have seen every episode of the original series dozens of times and can call out the lines before they are spoken. Yet they continue to watch religiously because *Star Trek* provides for them a likable vision of the future.

In this vision technology and human intelligence have triumphed, war on earth has been banished by the uniting of all nations under one government, and earthlings have marshaled their resources to reach out to life on other planets—even allowing the half-Vulcan Mr. Spock to be second in command of the starship *Enterprise.*

Many of the challenges met by the *Enterprise's* crew involve mystical and occult encounters. Irving Hexham and Karla Poewe, in *Understanding Cults and New Religions*, point out that when the program was first shown, belief in the occult was low, but by putting these things off into the future, the producers were able to bring disembodied spirits and other occult phenomena into their scripts (p. 29).

The Eastern-oriented mystical philosophy that was taking over Hollywood at this time was displayed even more prominently in *Star Wars*, the most popular movie of the early 1970s. While Luke Skywalker may have been the hero of *Star Wars* and its sequels, it was the power of "the Force," which Yoda (a character obviously based on an Eastern guru) taught him to use, that gave him victory. And it was the returning spirit of the deceased Obi Wan Kanobi that taught him to rely on "the Force."

While these programs were known to be science *fiction*, fans of both will tell you with avid enthusiasm that the things portrayed in them are all scientifically possible—just give us a little more time to develop the technology. (This widely held belief is manifestly false. The first premise on which virtually all science fiction is based is the ability to travel faster than the speed of light. Science knows of no way of transporting matter above the subatomic level even *at* the speed of light, let alone beyond.)

In 1976 the *In Search of . . .* television series began to be broadcast. These programs, along with a series of paperback books based on them, popularized exploration of occult and mystical phenomena such as witchcraft, communication with extraterrestrials, and devil worship.

How much influence movies and TV programs have on the beliefs of viewers is a much-debated subject. Clearly, though, these programs have affected the way people think about the universe. A Gallup survey taken in 1966 revealed that only 34 percent of Americans believed that there are beings similar to humans living on other planets; whereas 46 percent said they believed definitely that no such beings existed. When pollsters asked the same question in 1987, they discovered almost exactly opposite results—50 percent of respondents answered yes, while only 34 percent said no (A.J.S. Rayl, "UFO Poll," *Omni*, October 1987, p. 144).

Messages From Beyond

Interplanetary communication was not limited to moon trips and television fantasies during the sixties. People all over the world were reporting UFO sightings, and some even claimed to have received telepathic communications from the beings who piloted the craft. Not surprisingly, these purported extraterrestrials delivered messages about a coming new age of peace when all the world would cooperate—just as on *Star Trek*.

Arthur Ford, meanwhile, was relaying messages from the "other side" that purported to come from dozens of people who had died and gone on to the spirit realms. His spirit guides taught him that the New Age was to be brought in by a leader from the East because the Holy City of Revelation has gates on every side, but the teacher must come through the eastern gate. Ford's guides interpreted the influx of ideas from Eastern mysticism as indications of the coming of the New Age, and even went so far as to tell one man he was to be the teacher who would bring in the New Age—more about that in chapter 8 (Arthur Ford, *Unknown But Known*, pp. 121, 122). Raymond A. Moody's popular book *Life After Life*, published in 1976, lent what many people accepted as scientific credence to Ford's teaching that death is only a door to another realm.

Ford's foremost protégé is Ruth Montgomery, whom he encouraged to attempt automatic writing. In automatic writing a person says a prayer in which he or she opens up himself or herself to be used by any spirit entity that may want to communicate. The suppliant holds a pencil loosely in the hand on a blank piece of paper.

Montgomery, a widely known and respected Washington, D.C., political columnist, became involved with the psychic world through her interest in Jeanne Dixon. Her biography of Dixon was the *Reader's Digest* condensed book in July 1965.

Montgomery first tried automatic writing in 1960 after Ford told her she had a gift for it. She describes her experience of learning to take advantage of the gift in the 1986 book *Ruth Montgomery: Herald of the New Age*. After trying for a few minutes each morning, she would give up, but then "at last, on the tenth morning, some otherworldly force of herculean strength seemed to grasp my hand, and although my eyes were closed, it propelled the pencil into circles and figure eights with such pressure that I thought the lead point would break. I could not have dropped it if I'd tried."

The next day the pencil began to deliver messages from Ruth's deceased father. Soon other deceased relatives began to draw pictures and send messages. Next a spirit mentor named Lily took over and began to relay "beautiful philosophy" through Ruth's pencil. Then Lily told Ruth to try typing. When her fingers began to produce words automatically at her typewriter, the beautiful philosophy—including information about reincarnation and life after death—came in a torrent (pp. 3, 4). So far the torrent has yielded 10 or more books full of messages from persons Montgomery refers to as her "guides." Several of the books have hit the best-seller lists, and all have sold very well.

Montgomery's guides have much to say about the coming New Age. They continually repeat that sometime before the turn of the century the earth will tilt on its axis, causing major catastrophes, killing the majority of people on Earth, and destroying civilization as we now know it.

In *Aliens Among Us* Montgomery wrote that her guides had told her to believe the messages that have been coming to other psychics from purported extraterrestrials who claim to live in spaceships that are circling our planet. When the earth shifts on its axis, the enlightened people (presumably New Age believers) will be rescued by spaceships.

Note the similarity between the description of the spaceships' rescue mission given by a psychic called Tuella and the biblical description of the second coming of Jesus. "The Great Evacuation will come upon the world very suddenly. The flash of emergency events will be as the lightning that flashes in the sky [cf. Matthew 24:27]. Our rescue ships will be able to come in close enough in the twinkling of an eye [see 1 Corinthians 15:52] to set the lifting beams in operation in a moment. Mankind will be lifted [see 1 Thessalonians 4:17], levitated shall we say, by the beams from our smaller ships. These smaller craft will in turn taxi the persons to the larger ships overhead, higher in the atmosphere, where there is ample space and quarters and supplies for millions of people" (Montgomery, *Aliens Among Us*, pp. 51, 52). After the crisis brought on by the shift of axis is past, these enlightened ones will be set down on the earth again (cf. Revelation 21:10) to usher in the New Age of peace and harmony.

It's in the Stars

During the sixties also, belief in astrology began to be resurrected. Although the revelation in early 1988 that First Lady Nancy Reagan had allowed an astrologer to guide the shaping of the president's schedule created quite a stir in the press, the story really was not surprising. A recent Gallup poll revealed that 80 million Americans regularly consult an astrology column.

Astrology has a major contribution to make in preparing people to expect the New Age to be just around the corner. Everyone who was within earshot of a radio in the late 1960s or early 1970s had the New Age hope indelibly impressed on his or her mind as the words "this is the dawning of the age of Aquarius" blared from radios tuned to popular music stations.

The dawning of the age of Aquarius is just another name for the coming of the New Age. As Ruth Montgomery explains: "Planet Earth is currently on the cusp between the Piscean and Aquarian Ages. . . . We are indeed on the threshold of a New Age, which the Guides say will be ushered in by a shift of the earth on its axis at the close of this century" (*Threshold to Tomorrow*, p. 248).

Just before his death in 1983 Johnny Lister, a nationally syndicated astrology columnist, wrote a book entitled *The New Age*. In it he shared his belief that "the coming of the Aquarian age is an unprecedented time in modern history. . . . By being here at this time we have one of the greatest opportunities ever" (pp. 35-37).

Astrologers make much of the fact that the transition that is occurring right now is taking the world out of the Piscean age, represented by a fish, the early Christian symbol of Christ. They note also that astrological ages last just over 2,000 years and that the Piscean age began at the time of Christ. They believe that the Aquarian age will be characterized more by peace because of the decline of the influence of Christianity.

Astrologer Dane Rudhyar, author of the book *Occult Preparations for a New Age*, has calculated that the transition from the Piscean to the Aquarian age will take a total of 216 years, divided into three segments of 72 years each. The transition began in 1846. The first phase was completed in 1918. At that time the second phase, which was "marked by the rise of the Soviet Union and the vast increase in power of the counterbalancing United States of America," began. This second phase will end in 1990; but Rudhyar is less free with predictions of what that will mean than he is with interpretations of what past transitions yielded. Perhaps in the future this will be linked to the relaxation of trade barriers between the nations of the European economic community. That step is scheduled to occur in 1992. The transition to the Aquarian age will not be astrologically complete until 2062 (D. Rudhyar, *The*

Astrology of America's Destiny, p. 205).

All of these influences coming out of the 1960s and early 1970s continue to impact our culture as we head into the 1990s. While some of these influences have had little or no direct connection with the New Age movement as it now appears, they all had a heavy impact in preparing people to be receptive to the ideas that today are lumped together under the New Age heading.

I have dealt with these particular influences because they were among the strongest in changing the way people view life and their perception of how one should arrive at conclusions about what is true or false, right or wrong. All of them are instrumental in preparing people to accept New Age teachings.

Now at the end of the 1980s the paradigm shift has already taken place for a vast number of Americans. They are ready and waiting for revelations that will help them to make the transition to the long-awaited New Age.

Revelations toward that end abound today. But before we accept them wholeheartedly, we need to know something about their source.

CHAPTER
4

The Spirit Smorgasbord

It was the end of a hard week, and Jach Pursel was tired. The long days of high-powered executive training classes had drained him of energy. He needed to relax, and he knew just how to do it. Easing into a chair in his hotel room, he closed his eyes, took a deep breath, and began the process of relaxation that would lead him into transcendental meditation.

As a relaxation technique TM had always worked well for Jach, but he'd never noticed much benefit beyond that. He usually fell asleep after relaxing for only a few minutes. But not this time.

"All of a sudden, vivid imagery began," he says. "It was early evening. Dense forest, somewhat dark. I was walking along a path and came to a brook. . . .

"I turned around and saw a log cabin with a thatched roof nestled in the trees. . . . I walked up the steps, opened the door, and went in. A man dressed in white robes was standing next to a counter; behind him a blackboard and to the side a fire lit in a fireplace. I said hello. He said hello. I asked him his name, and he said, 'Lazaris.' Then he started talking about all kinds of things—reality and how we create it" (Katharine Martin, "The Voice of Lazaris," *New Realities*, July-August 1987, p. 28).

When he came out of his meditative state, Jach was astounded at what he had seen and heard. But he didn't attach any special meaning to it—he thought he might have imagined the whole thing, although he didn't dismiss it as a dream.

Things might not have gone any further if it hadn't been for his wife, Peny. When Jach told her about his encounter, it rang certain bells in her mind. She had been reading the works of Edgar Cayce, the "sleeping prophet" who diagnosed people's illnesses and spoke on a multitude of metaphysical subjects while in a trance, and Jane Roberts, author of several books based on material spoken through her by a spirit entity called Seth.

Peny wouldn't let Jach brush the whole thing off as a fluke. She kept encouraging him to pursue the matter further, but Lazaris had told Jach, "When it's time, I'll contact you again; don't try to contact me" (*ibid.*). All subsequent attempts to contact Lazaris proved fruitless for several months. But then Peny got Jach to try question and answer meditation. Jach seemed to fall asleep during the meditation—ending one answer in midsentence. But his mouth continued to move, and now a voice, different in tone and accent from his own, began to speak through him. It was Lazaris!

Jach and Peny weren't quite sure what to make of Lazaris' messages—whether they were just coming from within Jach's own mind or what. Significantly, when they wanted to consult with someone, they selected a man who was "steeped in Eastern philosophy and metaphysical mysticism" (*ibid.*, p. 31).

During the intervening years Lazaris has refined his transmission technique, now speaking through Jach on a regular basis, which earns Jach a handsome income. According to *Time*, Pursel charges an average of $700 a year to the long list of regular customers who come to consult Lazaris—not to mention the fees for workshops attended by hundreds of avid Lazaris fans. "Yeah, a lot of money gets made," Jach Pursel told one reporter ("New Age Harmonies," *Time*, Dec. 7, 1987, p. 66).

Among his customers are many of the rich and famous of Hollywood and Beverly Hills. Shirley MacLaine may be the most noted of his customers, but Lazaris got a special publicity boost when Sharon Gless, costar of the television series *Cagney and Lacey*, won the Emmy Award for best actress. In her acceptance speech she gave the credit for her success to Lazaris (Alexander, "Theology From the Twilight Zone," *Christianity Today*, Sept. 18, 1987, p. 22). Other stars who come by regularly include Michael York, Lesley Ann Warren, Ted Danson, and Colin Higgins (Martin, p. 27).

Lots of Love

And what sorts of messages do the listeners receive from this spirit entity? Lazaris loves to talk about love. "You can grow through love and joy and laughter, which is closer to the voice of God/Goddess/All That Is than any other sound you can imagine," he says in words reminiscent of 1 John 4:16 (*ibid.*, p. 32).

But mixed in with this wonderful, warm message are a lot of ideas and concepts that directly contradict the Bible.

For example, Lazaris identifies himself as a spirit

entity who communicates with many other spiritual entities who do not have bodies. He says that he has chosen to work through Pursel because he has observed Pursel through several lifetimes, which have aligned him properly to receive the transmissions. Peny also had experiences in previous lives that made Lazaris want to contact her.

Lazaris' mission includes helping with the unfolding of the New Age—a time of evolution to new levels of consciousness. "We want to help you evolve to the point that you co-create reality with us, your Higher Self, ultimately with God/Goddess/All That Is," he says (*ibid.*, p. 33).

Lazaris is certainly not alone in proclaiming his intent to channel messages through human beings to help to bring in the New Age.

David Spangler's book *Revelation: The Birth of a New Age* is based on transmissions he received from a spirit entity with the alluring name Limitless Love and Truth (LL&T). "I am timeless and infinite," LL&T says. "Am I God? Am I a Christ? Am I a Being come to you from the dwelling places of the Infinite? I am all these things, yet more. I am the very life of you and there is not one creature upon this planet but what expresses me and yearns for me more fully. I am Life but I am not a Being. I contain all Beings" (p. 60). LL&T gave Spangler six "transmissions" dealing with the coming of the New Age.

Spangler spent many years propagating and publishing LL&T's messages as well as messages from another spirit entity called John. Spangler started the Lorian Association in the United States, and the Lorian Press published his book *Revelation*. But Spangler just may be coming to doubt the reliability of the spirits' transmissions. In an article titled "Defining the New

Age," which serves as the introduction to the 1988 edition of *The New Age Catalogue*, Spangler wrote: "Seeing psychics and their prophecies come and go over the years with a minimal record of accuracy, I have generally learned to disregard them in favor of the potentialities of the immediate moment."

But other channels have by no means been dissuaded in the same way. Nor have publishers become discouraged with rushing into print new titles based on the channeled transmissions. Over the past year I have watched these books multiply in my favorite bookstores. In a recent visit to the Seattle area I discovered a bookstore with a New Age and occult (the two are generally regarded as synonymous) section 15 feet long and 7 feet high! One New Age book distributor in the United States recently reported that he is now distributing a total of 17,000 titles and has 3,200 bookstores on his customer list (see "Demystifying New Age Books," *Publishers Weekly*, June 24, 1988, pp. 58, 60).

Ramtha is one of the popular beings that speaks through a channel. A recent book by or about him is dedicated to "The I Am That We All Are" (*I Am Ramtha*, dedication page). In order to channel Ramtha, J. Z. Knight, an attractive housewife and horse breeder who lives in Yelm, Washington, says that she goes through an experience similar to that which is reported by people who "die" on an operating table or in an accident but are later revived. Her soul, she says, passes "to another plane of existence via an astral excursion" (Ramtha with Douglas James Mahr, *Voyage to the New World*, p. 16). When this happens, "the softness of J. Z.'s mannerisms and facial expressions are replaced by those of a man; body postures and gestures are surging with power; his concentration becomes an intensity, the voice is that of another knowingness" (*ibid.*, p. 17).

There is considerable evidence to indicate that this particular manifestation comes not from any truly supernatural source, but is merely the product of Knight's acting ability. Yet because Knight attracts thousands of disciples who take her Ramtha utterances for gospel truth, and because the manifestation speaks about the New Age, I have chosen to deal with it, using the designation Ramtha/Knight.

The New Bible

Barbara Marx Hubbard, a popular speaker and author who describes herself as a futurist, is not a channel per se. She would no doubt rather be known as a researcher with expertise in channeling. New Age magazines advertise a videotape titled *The Complete Guide to Channeling*, in which Hubbard interviews various channels and advises viewers on all the do's and don'ts of channeling.

But Hubbard's interest in such things arose from a personal experience that can only be described as channeling.

One day while out for a drive in California she noticed a sign pointing to "Mount Calvary." She felt and responded to an urgent compulsion to follow the road, and found an Episcopal monastery at the top of a hill. During her visit a voice began dictating to her a message about the high state of evolution of certain souls on earth. The voice also told about the impending transformation of our world as more and more people come into alignment with God and evolve from *Homo sapiens* into *Homo universalis* (Barbara Marx Hubbard, *Happy Birthday Planet Earth*, pp. 8, 9).

Hubbard checked into the monastery as a guest for

a silent retreat, and while there she wrote an interesting reinterpretation of the New Testament to bring its message into harmony with the futurist New Age teachings that were being transmitted to her.

Kevin Ryerson probably gets as much attention as any individual channel today because of his association with actress Shirley MacLaine, whom *Time* magazine describes as "the New Age's reigning whirling dervish" ("New Age Harmonies," Dec. 7, 1987, p. 63) because of her high visibility and heavy involvement in promoting the mystical side of the New Age movement. Ryerson channels at least four different entities, the most popular of whom calls himself John and speaks in what Ryerson describes as biblical lingo. I have seen no indication that the John he channels claims to be the same one channeled by David Spangler. (It is quite common for spirit entities to take names reminiscent of people mentioned in the Bible, but to deliver messages that have little correlation with the book of the Bible that bears that name.)

In a recent trip to a bookstore I glanced through a 1986 book whose channeled author identified himself simply as "the Christ." Commenting on the Creation story, "Christ" noted parenthetically that "Hindu teachings are more useful about this than the Jewish and Christian religions, of course" (Virginia Essene, ed., *New Teachings for an Awakening Humanity*, p. 24).

Maybe "Christ" didn't realize he had been beaten to the punch by a being calling himself Emmanuel (one of the biblical names of Christ—see Matthew 1:23), whose book titled simply *Emmanuel's Book* was published in 1985 by the New Age department of Bantam Books. Pat Rodegast serves as channel for Emmanuel's discourses.

Both of these beings were actually way behind the

spirit who identified himself as "Jesus" to Helen Schucman, a Jewish psychology professor at Columbia University. One day in 1965 this spirit voice came into her mind and announced, "This is a course in miracles. Please take notes" (Judith Skutch, in John White, "A Course in Miracles: Spiritual Wisdom for the New Age," *Science of Mind*, March 1986, pp. 10-14, 80-88).

Over the next 11 years the notes for the course continued to come into Schucman's mind, not audibly, but as "rapid inner dictation which I took down in a shorthand notebook" (*The New Age Catalogue*, p. 7).

Despite claiming to be dictated by Jesus, the course teaches that "The Son of God . . . is not Jesus but our combined Christ consciousness" (White, pp. 10-14, 80-88). The course, now published as an 1,100-page book, is widely read among New Age believers, and even many Christians recommend it despite its opposition to the biblical view of Jesus.

But all these pseudobiblical messengers, though they may claim to be eternal, are relative newcomers on the earth scene. The Swiss psychoanalyst Carl Jung claimed for years to carry on communications with a being called Philemon, whom Jung identified as merely "an archetypal figure in his own unconscious" (Raymon Van Over, in Jane Roberts, *The Seth Material*, p. xvii). But perhaps the most widely known spirit communicator to claim a biblical name was Seth, who was channeled by Jane Roberts from the early 1960s until her death in 1984. Roberts' accounts of Seth's messages were the first supernaturally dictated writings to become widely read in recent years.

Among other spirits who speak today are Ambres, who transmits medical and other information through a Swedish carpenter in Stockholm, the first spirit being Shirley MacLaine heard speak; Mentor, who sends messages to Meredith Lady Young, whom he has renamed Agartha, based on a Sanskrit word meaning "heaven bound"; the guides who work through automatic writing with Ruth Montgomery; and unnamed spirit entities who communicated the material in *The Starseed Transmissions—An Extraterrestrial Report* to Ken Carey, who has recently taken the name Raphael.

Fairies and Computers

R. Ogilvie Crombie, mentioned in chapter 2 in connection with the Findhorn community, is a channel of a different sort. Rather than receiving messages telepathically from unseen entities, he likes to talk face to face with beings such as the god Pan and various fauns, fairies, and gnomes.

Perhaps the most unusual channel is a computer in the Soviet Union. I read about it in a source (a tabloid newspaper) whose veracity I cannot vouch for, but the story is interesting and I share it simply as an illustration of a point that I have seen verified in other places: research into the supernatural is being pursued even by supposedly atheistic governments. Citing an article in a publication called *The Paranormal Studies*, the *Weekly World News* of May 31, 1988, tells about a group of scientists, including Dr. Pyater Suslov, at the University of Tashkent in the Soviet Union who have programmed a computer to receive messages from the dead. The computer is connected to an apparatus designed to detect minute fluctuations in electrical fields. The scientists taught terminally ill patients a computer code in hopes that once they were dead they could send messages back to the computer. After 13 years of trying, they are now receiving messages they believe come from a man called Comrade K. He was the thirty-seventh of their trainees to die, and it took several weeks after he died before the communications purportedly coming from him began to register on the computer.

The UFO Connection

High on the list of best selling books for 1987 was *Communion*, by Whitley Strieber, a well-known science fiction writer. But *Communion* was on the nonfiction list. The book's subtitle: "A True Story."

Strieber tells the story of his having discovered, through hypnosis, that the cause of certain unexplained marks on his body and of the severe depression he was going through was an abduction that he could remember only under hypnosis.

And this was no ordinary abduction. Strieber believes that he was taken out of his cabin in upstate New York on December 26, 1985, and taken aboard some sort of flying craft. While on board he was subjected to a physical examination by insect-like creatures about three and a half feet tall. The exam memories could easily be brushed off as a mere dream were it not for the fact that he had an infected finger and a scab near his ear. The simplest explanation of their existence are the events that occurred during the exam that he subsequently "remembered" under hypnosis.

Strieber's story, which several hundred thousand people must have read by now, has no direct connection with the New Age movement. But the fact that it could have been published and sold in such large numbers in recent years does bear relation to the movement. Because visits by and messages from UFOs play a large part in some people's expectations for the New Age.

The book *Seeds of Tomorrow: New Age Communities*

That Work, published by Harper and Row in 1984, reports on 15 different communes, or communities, around the world, including Findhorn in Scotland and the Universal Brotherhood located up the west coast of Australia from Perth.

Members of the Universal Brotherhood believe that "extraterrestrial 'elder brothers' in flying saucers are telepathically assisting humanity to expand its consciousness." The earth is about to be destroyed; but prior to the destruction, these brothers—under the command of "Jesus of Nazareth, the sovereign ruler of this local universe and the commander of the UFO space fleet"—will evacuate all people "who have demonstrated that they are worth saving" (p. 111). Some may regard the Universal Brotherhood as a group of crackpots. Others point out that despite their affirmation of Jesus they are teaching a very non-Christian form of salvation by works. But its members have attracted enough attention that John Denver, in Australia for a performance in Perth, made a special airplane trip to their community.

And Australia certainly is not the only place where people believe they are receiving transmissions from space brothers. Previously mentioned in chapter 3 was Tuella, who believes she receives transmissions from the Ashtar Command. In 1971 Brad Steiger, who is widely regarded as one of the world's foremost authorities on flying saucer accounts, edited a book entitled *The Aquarian Revelations*. Although Steiger wrote most of the book, he was credited only as the editor, apparently because the copyright is held by Robin McPherson and Eugene Olson.

An interesting story lies behind the revelations in this book. Robin's mother, a longtime "student of the occult and various esoteric doctrines" (Brad Steiger, ed., *The Aquarian Revelations*, p. 23) ("esoteric doc-trines" refers probably to the writings of the Theo-sophical Society and Alice Bailey), saw a flying saucer one night in early 1969. She quickly called Robin, and though the saucer had disappeared before Robin came, it soon reappeared and hovered for her benefit. It then climbed swiftly and disappeared. Soon there-after Robin began to channel messages from a space entity who identified himself as OX-HO and signed off at the end of his transmissions with the name Adonai Vassu. Steiger, who had been investigating reputed flying saucer contactees for three years, considered this contact significant enough to devote most of a book to it. As might be expected, OX-HO had much to say about the coming New Age.

While on the surface there seems to be little simi-larity between what Strieber believes happened to him and Robin McPherson's telepathic contact with UFO inhabitants, the differences are only superficial.

Both types of contact appear to be designed to lead people to believe that intelligent beings who are more highly evolved than earthlings exist in outer space.

The OX-HO type of contact appeals to those who are open to telepathic communications from friends in outer space. But for those who scoff at such things, stories such as *Communion* seem to portray more rational evidence for believing in highly evolved space beings.

In the end it matters not which story you prefer. Both lead to much the same conclusions about the nature of life in our universe.

Channels and Shamans

In reading about channels and how they operate, I began to notice certain characteristics common to them all. And that set me to thinking about something else that I had researched at the Library of Congress.

I had looked into the topic of shamanism only because I had noticed frequent references to American Indian and other shamans in New Age publications. For example, prime reading among New Age believers are books by Carlos Castaneda, who claims to have studied under a Mexican Indian shaman named Don Juan. New Age writers who are concerned about holistic health—that is, with treating the whole person rather than just one symptom—also have much to say about shamans and what we can learn from them.

If you're wondering what a shaman is, maybe the term *witch doctor* or *medicine man* is more familiar to you. Most stories about Indians and other primitive peoples refer to the village shaman as the witch doctor or medicine man.

Shamanism is a worldwide phenomenon among traditional cultures. The word *shaman* itself is said to have been derived from one of two possible origins. Either from a Sanskrit word referring to a Buddhist monk or from a word meaning "he who knows" (Joseph Campbell, *The Way of the Animal Powers*, vol. 1, p. 157). The word *shaman* itself is used only by the Tungu people of eastern Siberia, but it has been adopted in modern times to denote the phenomenon as it is found in cultures throughout the world.

Spencer L. Rogers, professor emeritus of anthropology at San Diego State University, divides shamans into two types. "In the case of the *inspirational*, or *ecstatic* type, of shaman, the spirits speak through the shaman, and the messages are interpreted to the people by an assistant. The shaman himself later may have no memory of the content of the message. With the other type of shaman, which has been termed a *seer*, the spirits speak to the shaman and he, in turn, relays the messages to the people" (*The Shaman*, p. 6).

Reading accounts of sessions with various channels and comparing them with what I had learned about shamans convinced me that the modern channeling phenomenon is similar in many ways to shamanism, especially ecstatic shamanism.

Shamans operate on the assumption that unseen spirits exist and can communicate with us. So do channels.

Shamans typically receive their communications from spirits while in a trance state. So do channels.

Shamans often go through a lengthy ritual to achieve the trance state. Modern channels have developed techniques more suited to what I call the push-button, pop-pill generation, which wants instant answers. They can enter a trance after only a few minutes of meditation.

Shamans often do not recall having said what they said while in the trance. Ditto for channels.

The shaman is typically a person who had a traumatic experience during childhood, which led to a change of personality (Campbell, p. 156). Margo Chandley, a doctoral student doing research on channeling, found that of the 13 channels she studied, 12 had had a traumatic experience in childhood that had caused them to withdraw from society and look inward for answers (Lynn Smith, "The New, Chic Metaphysical Fad of Channeling," Los Angeles *Times*, Dec. 5, 1986).

Most shamans serve their tribe with medical and health-sustaining information. Most channels today do the same.

People consult a shaman when their naturalistic,

humanistic solutions are inadequate. The same is true of channels.

Ecstatic shamans work closely with and are supportive of Hinduism and Buddhism. Rogers notes that most shamans in Asia are of the ecstatic type. Modern channels are supportive of Hindu and Buddhist concepts of life—as opposed to the biblical view.

Shamans almost always oppose Christian teachers who come to their village. Modern channels manifest their opposition by contradicting the teachings of the Bible.

Are channels, then, just modern shamans who have come on the scene to meet the needs of a postmodern people who, disillusioned with technological solutions, have gone looking for answers more satisfying to their primitive needs?

That may be part of the reason channeling has become such a widespread phenomenon. But I think there are other reasons of equal importance.

An important question is What is the source of the messages coming through the channels? It hardly seems likely, based on the type of knowledge channels such as Kevin Ryerson relay (often including intimate details known only to a listener), that the information comes from within the channel's own mind.

What I have shared in this chapter about channels barely scratches the surface. I have mentioned only a few of the most notable channels and their entities. Every time I read an article about channeling, I learn of one or two more additional channels that are active today.

In the next two chapters we will take up the questions of why channels are so abundant today, what their relationship is to the New Age movement, and where their messages come from.

CHAPTER
5

Channels and the New Age

Channeling is important to the New Age movement for two reasons. First of all, the movement draws upon the basic craving of humans to communicate with spirits beyond their own. At the foundation of the movement is a sense that technological society, which used to be viewed as the panacea for earth's ills, is too impersonal and too neglectful of the needs of the human psyche.

The second reason that channeling is important is that all of the newly communicative entities support the idea that earth and its inhabitants are on the verge of a new age of enlightenment, spirituality, and peace.

Thus a person who identifies with the New Age hope is usually open to the channeled messages. Typically, New Age-oriented people who are involved with channeling have longed for something spiritual, and the spirits who speak in terms of the New Age hope address a topic that already appeals to the hearts of these searchers.

Unfortunately, the process of reasoning that leads

to this openness to channeled messages is dangerous, founded as it is on a faulty method of arriving at truth. It therefore sets up a person to receive flawed or manipulated data, and hence to be led to wrong conclusions.

You should not ask a car salesman whether or not you need to buy a new car. You should not ask the president of R. J. Reynolds Tobacco Company whether or not you should quit smoking. At least not if you want an unbiased answer.

Do you see the analogy? If you want to be persuaded that you need a new car, then perhaps the best person to consult *is* a car salesman. But if you're looking for an unbiased opinion about your automotive needs, you'll likely get a more balanced opinion from a friend or a mechanic who does not have a profit motive for persuading you to buy.

To go out looking for spiritual encouragement that the New Age is about to dawn and then to latch on to whichever spirit comes along proclaiming that hope is to set yourself up for deception. It is to set yourself up to be victimized by any spirit or shyster whose purposes are served by feeding you the line you want to hear. •

Feeling Good About Yourself

Corrinne McLaughlin made this point in an article that was published as part of a special channeling section in *New Realities* magazine in 1987. "A further explanation for the popularity of channels now," she wrote, "is that they tell people all the things their egos always wanted to hear: you can have anything you want; you deserve it; you're perfect just as you are, so you don't have to try harder to be a better person, etc."

("Tuning In to the Best Channel," *New Realities*, July-August 1987, p. 38).

Although the overall tone of this article, and of the magazine's special channeling section, was positive toward channeling, at one point McLaughlin advises: "The only really sure way to avoid getting false information or being deceived or controlled by a psychic or channel—don't consult one in the first place!" (*ibid.*, p. 41).

A good example of a person who set herself up for deception by a channel is Shirley MacLaine. She first became involved with channeling when she was going through a deep crisis. First she watched a channel in action. On the basis of the seemingly supernatural source of his messages—and the messages' apparently beneficent nature—she decided that the messages must be coming from an entity with the good of its listeners at heart. Then she began to seek other channels to help her understand her crisis. And not only her crisis, but the deep questions about whether God exists, whether or not humans have souls, and what happens after death.

She thought she could make her contacts with channeled entities on the level of detached research. But when Tom McPherson, one of the entities channeled by Kevin Ryerson, revealed that he not only knew that she was having a secret affair with a prominent politician but also the very words that the man she was involved with had said to her recently, she was caught off guard and felt compelled to become a true believer in channeled entities. Then the entity John, also channeled by Ryerson, revealed that he also knew about her affair and proceeded to answer the question she most needed answered.

That question was Why did she and Gerry, the

married man with whom she was having the affair, have such an attraction for each other? John answered her question before she even asked it by explaining that she and Gerry had been married in a previous life.

MacLaine bought it. What else could she do? The speaking entity had swept away her defenses by revealing that he knew about her secret affair. And now he offered her a justification for the affair that helped her shut off the last vestige of a nagging conscience that had questioned whether what she was doing was right.

Shirley MacLaine quickly bit the hook of channeling. And since that time she has done more to promote channeling and New Age thinking than any other person on earth. Her best-selling book *Out on a Limb*, in which she tells the story of her first contacts with Ambres, Tom, and John, was made into a television miniseries that first aired in early 1987. Now Ms. MacLaine has written two more best-sellers detailing her further explorations into the occult.

Much of the current interest in channeling can be traced to the *Out on a Limb* miniseries, not only because of the number of people who watched it but because it was the first blatant broaching of the subject of channeling in a nonfiction environment on television. It opened the television channels to channeling. B. Dalton bookstores reported that sales of books on occult topics nearly doubled during the week that it was shown.

Channel Jane Roberts told similar stories of people coming to her in time of need and leaving convinced that she was indeed in communication with a beneficent spirit called Seth. In *The Seth Material*, for example, she tells about a young couple who were distraught over the death of their 3-year-old son. They came to her seeking to understand why such a seemingly perfect child should die so young. Seth channeled through with the message that their son's soul had come to be with them and help them only for a short time. He had come to repay a debt from his father's previous life when the father had helped the son's soul. The son had come back to live a short life and then die suddenly to bring the father to seek answers about the nature of life. And now, voila! Here they were seeking—just what he had hoped they would do! The couple found this message so comforting that they could not help becoming ardent defenders of Seth *and* everything he said about the nature of life.

The Danger of Deception

Many New Age-oriented people recognize the danger of deception inherent in seeking spirit guides while using the main criterion that they must agree with what one already believes or wants to believe. Theodore Roszak, the historian introduced in chapter 2, for example, warned in his book *Unfinished Animal* that there are dangers involved in the carnival atmosphere that accompanies many people's spiritual search.

There is, he wrote, "one final danger of the carnival. Every religious tradition warns us at some point of the perils of demonic interception. We do not wander into these strange regions without risking mind and spirit both. Lucifer, so tradition teaches us, was once a prince of light. Can we safely assume he has forgotten how to set us false beacons or to dazzle us with many a pyrotechnic display? If, in salvaging the outlawed spiritual teachings of human culture, we are to take their wisdom seriously, then we can hardly ignore the symbol of the great trickster who is also a god—but god upside down. *Demon deus inversus est"* (p. 71).

This observation is especially significant because it comes from an author whose thesis is that we humans are, indeed, on the verge of a New Age in which we will reach unsurpassed heights of excellence through taking charge of our own evolution.

Unfortunately, not all New Age thinkers are willing to reflect so discerningly about the spirits with which they seek contact. It is, after all, hard to think of someone as a liar when he or she is telling you exactly what you want to hear! But not to think discerningly about such messages means setting yourself up for deception.

Here, it seems to me, is the crux of an extremely important issue that anyone interested in the New Age movement must consider carefully. To ignore this issue and simply to accept messages that fit what you already want to believe is to set yourself up for deception and exploitation by any shyster who is willing to say what the listeners want to hear. To ignore this issue is to abandon the quest for true answers and to set oneself up as the ultimate judge of all truth. But when one sets himself or herself up as the supreme judge, then he or she does not need to consult a channel! A channel will be of no more value than any human counselor if one is not willing to accept everything he or she says as supernaturally revealed truth.

The Two Sources

Here is the issue. Two sources of information about the nature of our world and the meaning of life claim to have supernatural origin. But they teach the exact opposite of each other on *every* point of consequence about the nature of our world, the people who inhabit it, and the destiny of our planet.

You have only three possible responses to these alleged sources of revelation:

1. You can accept source A as authentic and trustworthy.

2. You can accept source B as authentic and trustworthy.

3. You can reject both and choose your own personal judgment and the judgment of other human beings as the only trustworthy guide for your decisions.

There are no in-between responses possible. If, for instance, you were to say that you would accept neither A nor B as totally authentic but would pick and choose and try to meld their messages together to arrive at truth, you would actually be making response 3.

If you totally reject responses 1 and 2, you accede to response 3 by default.

Most people's response, no matter what their religious persuasion, is number 3.

But in recent years, as more and more people have become disillusioned with human solutions to our world's problems, a craving for absolute answers from sources beyond the human has been rekindled.

In traditional societies the shaman, or witch doctor, typically supplies this need. He or she goes into a trance and receives enlightenment about where to hunt or how to cure a disease.

In the Western world the Bible (or the church in places where it has chosen to suppress the Bible) has fulfilled the role of supernatural guide.

On a whole, those areas of the world under the influence of Eastern religions accept response 3 without question when it comes to decisions about what is true and false, because Hindus and Buddhists hold that there is no such thing as absolute truth. But both Hinduism and Buddhism blend together well with primitive shamanism, so that when a need arises for supernatural healing or answers, the need is typically supplied by a shaman.

In the Muslim world the Koran, of course, supplies absolute answers. And for Jews, the Torah or *Tanakh*.

Craving for Answers

The past 10 years—a decade that saw the revival of Muslim fundamentalism in Iran and beyond, and the reassertion of evangelical fundamentalism in the United States—have witnessed a revival of interest in primitive shamanism under the name of channeling.

This is not surprising, for the three revivals all stem from the same sense of human insecurity. The same craving for answers beyond what human reasoning can supply lies behind these different yet common phenomena.

This is the craving that led Edgar Mitchell to found the Institute for Noetic Sciences after his trip to the moon. As Mitchell relates, the knowledge that the beauty of our world was not a mere accident of evolution came to him *noetically*. That is, it came to him intuitively—from within his psyche—rather than through the logical operations of mathematics or deductive reasoning.

The institute supports research into psychic phenomena, including channeling and shamanism. Although Mitchell himself does not think that channeled messages come from any supernatural source, nevertheless, what one thinks about the source of a message does not change its actual point of origin.

My own conclusion, after studying the messages coming from various New Age-oriented channels, is that a common source lies behind most of their messages. I do not believe that all—or even most—of the messages originate within the human mind.

I base my conclusion in part on the supernatural phenomena associated with the giving of the messages. These phenomena include the ability to speak a dialect otherwise unknown to the speaker, and the knowledge of secrets held only between a listener and a friend who has died or who is not present.

But my conclusion is based also on the fact that while there are broad areas of disagreement among today's channels about the specifics of the New Age, they all agree to disagree with the Bible. All the currently popular channels are relaying messages that are orchestrated to compel listeners to either accept the channel and reject the Bible or to reject the channel. And I believe that I know someone with supernatural powers who would like to keep people from believing the Bible. His name is Lucifer, or Satan, and he's the same being who channeled his message through a snake in the Garden of Eden.

The issue clearly comes down to a classic A or B decision. Despite the channels' claims to the contrary, one cannot accept the message of the Bible and the messages of the channels. They run contrary on every point of importance.

And this has led me to conclude that the reason so many channels touting the same antibiblical philosophy right now is that a grand scheme is gathering momentum, a grand scheme to bring about the great deception that the Bible predicts will lead almost everyone on earth to believe lies instead of truth just before the second coming of Jesus Christ. I have come to believe that perhaps God has been restraining these deceptive spirits until now, but that now He is finally allowing them to become active because He knows that time is short and that the final issue between truth and falsehood is soon to be decided once and for all.

The Bible Ban

The next chapter will deal with the various messages of the channels and will illustrate how they are contrary to the Bible. But in concluding this chapter, I want to note one characteristic that all the psychics and channels I have been able to get background information on, or whose messages I have studied, have in common. They all reject the Bible as God's revelation to human beings.

The line of modern channels can be traced back to the psychics of a few years ago. Most notable among these were Edgar Cayce and Arthur Ford. Both originally had a strong devotion to Christianity. Ford served at one time as a minister in the Christian Church. As a young man Cayce was a devoted Bible student. But during the course of their lives both men were seduced away from their biblical viewpoints by the psychic powers that took control of their lives. Eventually both Cayce and Ford rejected biblical teachings and accepted most of the same antibiblical ideas we will note among modern channels in the next chapter.

Among the modern channels I mentioned in the previous chapter, Jane Roberts testifies that though she was raised in a Catholic home, "before I was 20, then, I'd left behind me that archaic God, the Virgin, and the communion of saints. Heaven and hell, angels and devils, were dismissed. This particular group of chemicals and atoms I called 'me' would fall into no such traps—at least none that I could recognize" (*The Seth Material*, p. 6).

Meredith Lady Young, who wrote *Agartha*, a book based on messages received from a spirit being called Mentor, makes a point early in her book of mentioning her own spiritual path. It too included rejection of the Christian teachings she had once believed.

Alice Bailey, who channeled Djwhal Khul and whose writings are leading lights for many New Age thinkers, rejected her early Christian upbringing in favor of theosophy. Afterwards, she never again spoke with her own sister, who remained a Christian. Which side of the issue she was on is also obvious from the fact that she founded an organization called the Lucifer Trust.

Robin McPherson, who channeled the messages recorded in *The Aquarian Revelations*, was raised by a mother who "had long been a student of the occult and various esoteric doctrines" (p. 23), and Robin herself had attended a church only once and had never read the Bible.

Helen Schucman, who claimed to be a channel for "Jesus," was an atheist when she began to receive the messages she recorded.

And the computer in Russia never believed in God to start with!

Examination of the teachings of the rest of the channels will reveal that they too have rejected the Bible, though they may claim they have not.

CHAPTER
6

Whom to Believe

All of the currently and recently active channels that I have had opportunity to study agree on one thing—well, sort of agree, that is. They all agree that the New Age is either here already or coming soon. What they don't agree on is just how it will come about or what it will be like.

For years Ruth Montgomery's guides, for example, have been holding forth with the opinion that sometime before the year 2000 the earth will shift on its axis, causing immense floods as polar icecaps melt and totally disrupting civilization. As noted in chapter 3, they have now told her that certain enlightened beings from earth will be rescued by spaceships from the Ashtar Command and taken to other spaceships, in which they will be cared for until they can be put back on earth to usher in the New Age. Edgar Cayce's revelations confirm Montgomery's cataclysmic vision.

Limitless Love and Truth (LL&T), on the other hand, sending his (its?) messages through David Spangler, announces that "the new heaven and the new earth are forming in your midst." "The New Age does not require destruction to announce its arrival." "Earth itself, as a physical place, does not need to be cataclysmically altered in order to usher in the New Age" (*Revelation: The Birth of a New Age*, pp. 62, 165, 169).

Ramtha, channeled by J. Z. Knight, agrees with LL&T. In a question-and-answer session, a disciple posed this question: "Some of the sages and Edgar Cayce . . . have predicted grave disasters for the earth. Are these going to be so?"

Ramtha/Knight answered: "Because one sage predicted it the earth is going to crumble and be in despair of millions upon millions? No. . . . Now everyone expects for all these terrible things to happen—they shall not happen. They *never* will. . . .

"This place was built by Gods, collective ones. Every beautiful thing is continuously refining itself finer and finer. The New Age will continue on and be graceful without ever ending itself or losing itself" (*Voyage to the New World*, pp. 254-256).

According to Brad Steiger, who has studied the messages coming to numerous "UFO contactee" channels, the messages the "Space Brother" entities are sending indicate that the transition can go either way. One of the common threads in the messages is that *"man now stands in the transitional period before the dawn of a New Age.* With peace, love, understanding, and brotherhood on man's part, he will see a great new era begin to dawn" (*The Aquarian Revelations*, p. 12). But if we don't get our act together, *"severe earth changes and major cataclysms will take place.* Such disasters will not end the world, but shall serve as cataclysmic crucibles to burn off the dross of unreceptive humanity. Those who die in such dreadful purgings will be allowed to reincarnate on higher levels of development so that their salvation will be more readily accomplished through higher teachings on a higher vibratory level" (*ibid.*, p. 13).

But I think Lazaris, channeled by Jach Pursel, has the most creative way of sorting out the chances and making a prediction that can't go wrong. Building on the popular New Age conception that we all create our own reality by what we choose to think about, he says that people right now are choosing for themselves whether or not they will have to go through a cataclysm on the way to the New Age. "More and more people are choosing which world they want to live in, and the choice is more obvious than it has ever been before. At this point, each world can see the other. But in time, those worlds will separate: one a world of joy and the other a world of destruction, and they won't know each other or overlap. By that time, you'll be in one or the other" ("Lazaris on 1987," *New Realities*, July-August 1987, p. 29).

In other words, if you find yourself going through a cataclysm, it'll be your own fault, but if you manage to just drift right into the New Age, it'll be because you were enlightened and were thinking about the right things.

Zap '67

In 1967 a multitude of channeled entities (back then the people receiving the messages were called mediums or telepaths, not channels) all began to deliver the same message about just when the final cataclysm that would usher in the New Age would overtake us. John A. Keel reported that in 1967 "mediums, telepaths, sensitives, and UFO contactees throughout the world," many of whom did not even know of one

SECRETS OF THE NEW AGE

another's existence, all made the same prediction, even phrased the same in different languages: about midnight, December 24, a bright light would appear in the sky, and then—disaster (*UFOs—Operation Trojan Horse*, pp. 282, 283).

Keel, who does not believe that channels receive their messages from anywhere beyond earth, was so impressed with this particular phenomenon that he wrote: "The UFO contactees received the same identical messages as the trance mediums communing with spirits. . . . It was now clear (to me, anyway) that all of these people were tuned in to a central source" (*ibid.*, p. 283).

Of course, all of these people (and by extension, their sources) were wrong. But then, that's not unusual for channels and psychics. Ralph Blodgett has researched these things for many years, and in 1985 he used a computer to track the accuracy of 550 published predictions by psychics for that year. Of the 550, only 24 came true. That's less than 5 percent. In other words, 95 percent of what these supposed psychics were willing to go on record, in print, as predicting did not happen ("Can Psychics and Astrologers Predict the Future?" *Vibrant Life*, July-August 1986, p. 14).

Well, then, whom can you believe in all of this? The answer comes back to what we noted in the previous chapter. People tend to choose a channel who will tell them what they want to hear. And when they receive the message they've been looking for, they stick to that channel like flies to a cobweb.

Whom Should You Believe?

But when it comes down to a question of whom *should* you believe, you must take time for careful consideration before deciding. Remember the point I made in the previous chapter. If you're going to accept guidance from a supernatural source, you have to be able to believe implicitly in the trustworthiness of the source or the guidance is worthless. If you end up having to pick through a mountain of corn husks looking for a few kernels, you might as well give up and trust your own judgment of what's right in the first place and leave the channel alone.

Many supernatural entities are sending messages today. They cannot all be right. Why? Because they contradict each other. It's a simple matter of logic. Moreover, their predictions usually don't come true. Thus they are all demonstrably deceitful at worst or misled at best. But there is one thing on which they all agree. *They all agree that the Judaeo-Christian Scripture —the Bible—is wrong on some very important points.* One thing all these supernatural communicators want us to believe is that we cannot believe the Bible. They have mounted a massive propaganda campaign to malign its message.

From this fact alone, I think it is possible to form a meaningful hypothesis about the source of the channeled messages. All we have to do is ask Is there a supernatural power—a being or beings—that knows more than humans and thus is able to wow listeners by revealing facts that the listeners know are unknown to any other human? And if the answer is yes, do these entities have anything to gain by discrediting the Bible? If so, then that being (or beings) should head our list of possible sources. Don't you agree?

Remember Roszak's warning: "Lucifer, so tradition teaches us, was once a prince of light. Can we safely assume he has forgotten how to set us false beacons or to dazzle us with many a pyrotechnic display?" (*Unfinished Animal*, p. 71).

The Bible is the reliable source of our information about Lucifer, who is also known as Satan.

Think about that for a moment! Then think about this: If Adolf Hitler were suddenly to reappear on the scene and try to reassert his control over Germany, what would be the first thing he would have to accomplish? It only makes sense that he would have to destroy people's confidence in the history books that have revealed the evil results of following him in the past. Then he would want to reestablish himself as people's guide to what they should believe.

Can we expect Lucifer to be any less cunning than that?

I think not.

So let's examine the evidence to see whether the channels are indeed trying to discredit the Bible and its revelations about Lucifer's evil nature. Then we can decide whether to give Lucifer the credit for being the source of their messages.

Channels Versus the Bible

Every channel whose messages I have read contradicts the Bible on several important points.

They all preach cosmic evolution as the source of the human mind. They teach that spirits have been evolving for millions or billions of years, and that finally in human beings they have reached the level of consciousness and intentionality—the ability to make choices. This is the basis of their promise of the New Age soon to dawn—evolution is about to go one step further and bear fruit in beings on a still higher level, who will take better care of our earth. This evolution is also claimed to be the source of the channeled messages themselves, for the messengers claim to be more highly evolved beings living on higher planes or at higher vibrational levels.

The Bible, on the other hand, teaches that when human beings left Creator God's hand, they were perfect. Only because of sin have we reached the depths of degradation in which we now live. According to Scripture, humans have not been getting better and better through the millennia, but worse and worse as they have wandered further and further from God.

The channels all teach reincarnation. They teach that there is no such thing as death. A character in a book Richard Bach wrote after *Jonathan Livingston Seagull* comes back after being murdered to tell his friend that death at first is like diving into a cold lake on a hot day. The first few dives are shocking and invigorating, but after enough times it becomes old and easy—it's hardly even invigorating anymore.

The Bible teaches that the assurance "You will not surely die" was Satan's first lie (Genesis 3:4, NIV). It teaches that after death comes judgment. Those who have trusted God can look forward to resurrection, not reincarnation.

The channels all proclaim that Jesus of Nazareth was just one of many incarnations of a messenger sent from God.

The Bible teaches that Jesus is the unique (one-of-a-kind) Son of God who came to earth to live and die only once for all humanity. "For God so loved the world that he gave his *one and only Son*, that whoever believes in him shall not perish but have eternal life" (John 3:16, NIV). The King James Version translates the italicized words "only begotten Son." The Greek word does not mean that Jesus was an only child, but emphasizes that He was *unique*. That's why the translators of the New International Version rendered the term "one and only."

The channels either teach that there is no such thing as the devil, or Satan, or that he is really just a good angel who has gotten bad press in the Bible.

The Bible reveals that Satan is in his inmost nature a liar and the originator of all lies. Jesus says of the devil, or Satan: "There is no truth in him. When he lies, he speaks his native language, for he is a liar and the father of lies" (John 8:44, NIV).

The channels teach that there is no such thing as absolute truth or absolute deception. Everyone makes his or her own truth. This is called "pluralism" because it implies that there are plural truths rather than one singular truth—that what is true to one person may not be true to another who simply chooses to believe differently. In *The Closing of the American Mind*, one of the most widely read books of 1987, Allan Bloom pointed out that this is one of the most infectious and dangerous isms in America today.

The Bible calls Jesus *the* Way, *the* Truth, and *the* Life. It also records Jesus' promise that "you will know the truth, and the truth will set you free" (verse 32, NIV).

The channels teach that human beings are, by nature, either God or a part of God (their expression of this concept is one of the most confused, because at one time the same channel will teach that we are God, but at other times that we are only a part of God). They teach that we create our own reality and rule over it.

The Bible teaches that we are unique creatures of God, but are not God. He made us in His image (Genesis 1:26, 27), but we are distinct from Him. Scripture also asserts that only those who receive Jesus Christ as Saviour and Lord—those who thus become the children of God—will be granted the privilege of reigning with God *after* the second coming of Jesus. "Yet to all who received him, to those who believed in his name, he gave the right to become children of God" (John 1:12, NIV). "To him who overcomes, I will give the right to sit with me on my throne, just as I overcame and sat down with my Father on his throne" (Revelation 3:21, NIV).

The channels teach that human beings in and of themselves (or aided by more highly evolved souls like their own) have the power to overcome evil and make a perfect world.

The Bible teaches that apart from God human beings are powerless to do good. "All have turned aside, they have together become corrupt; there is no one who does good, not even one" (Psalm 14:3, NIV). However, through God's grace we can develop the kind of unselfish character that will make a perfect world possible. "This righteousness from God comes through faith in Jesus Christ to all who believe. There is no difference, for all have sinned and fall short of the glory of God, and are justified freely by his grace through the redemption that came by Christ Jesus" (Romans 3:22-24, NIV).

The channels teach that our hope for a better future should be founded on their predictions of the coming New Age when we will have evolved to a higher level.

The Bible teaches that our hope for a better future should be founded in God, who promises a new heaven and a new earth where those who trust in Jesus will be reunited with Him at Christ's second coming. "Nevertheless we, according to his promise, look for new heavens and a new earth, wherein dwelleth righteousness" (2 Peter 3:13). There we shall live in perfect peace, joy, health, and harmony. "And

I heard a loud voice from the throne saying, 'Now the dwelling of God is with men, and he will live with them. They will be his people, and God himself will be with them and be their God. He will wipe every tear from their eyes. There will be no more death or mourning or crying or pain, for the old order of things has passed away' " (Revelation 21:3, 4, NIV).

It all comes down to a simple choice. You can believe the Bible and be wary of channels. Or you can believe the channels and discard the Bible. But you can't believe both.

Whom should you believe? Before you decide to listen to a channel, take time to read the next chapter. You have nothing to lose.

If the Bible is right about Satan, you need to heed its warnings. If the channels are right, then you will be safe in believing them (or one of them, because you can't believe them all!). But you owe it to yourself to consider what the Bible says about Satan before you decide whether or not he is the likely source behind the channels.

CHAPTER
7

First Lie,
Final Lie

The Bible teaches that ever since the beginning of human history two forms of spirituality have been available to human beings.

Adam and Eve, the first two people God created, had the opportunity to communicate with God and imbibe of His Holy Spirit as He would come and walk in the Garden of Eden with them (see Genesis 3:8). The Holy Spirit was present on our earth even before God caused light to shine on and life to spring forth from our planet (see Genesis 1:2).

But even before God placed Adam and Eve in the Garden of Eden, war had broken out in—of all places—heaven! Revelation 12 divulges the details: Lucifer (Satan) led a band of angels in rebellion against God. When Satan's troops lost the war, they were cast out of heaven, down to the earth. "And there was war in heaven. Michael [another name for the preincarnate Christ] and his angels fought against the dragon, and the dragon and his angels fought back. But he was not strong enough, and they lost their place in heaven.

The great dragon was hurled down—that ancient serpent called the devil, or Satan, who leads the whole world astray. He was hurled to the earth, and his angels with him" (Revelation 12:7-9, NIV).

The reason Lucifer and his troops were allowed to come to the earth was that God wanted all His created beings to have free choice. He wanted Adam and Eve to choose for themselves whether they would serve God, or whether they would rebel against Him.

Satan and his rebellious troops now live on the earth, but because they are angelic in nature, they are not normally visible to us. They, like the angels who did not rebel, are spirit beings created with greater powers than those of humans. (Scripture identifies angels as spirit beings: "Are not all angels ministering spirits sent to serve those who will inherit salvation?" [Hebrews 1:14, NIV.]

These fallen angelic beings have powers we do not have. They can travel rapidly from place to place. They can communicate with one another instantly over long distances. They can create illusions. They can move physical objects. They can enter human minds through dreams and voices unless the mind is protected by God. They can take possession of human bodies that are not protected by God. They can cause illness. They can wreak havoc and destruction. They do not have physical bodies of their own that grow old and die. They listen in on our conversations without our even knowing they are there. They can remember what they hear and repeat it back later.

They can use their powers to deceive people—especially those who are unaware of their existence and purpose. Because they can move rapidly from place to place, they may appear to know what is happening in more than one place at a time. Or by acting in unison, they can even appear to be in more than one place at a time. By using their powerful memories along with their ability to create illusions, they can impersonate people who have died.

However, their powers are not unlimited. They cannot foresee the future, but they often can make better guesses than humans because they have been observing human nature and natural phenomena for thousands of years and so better understand the forces leading to events.

They cannot harm anyone without God's permission. But God has given them a certain amount of free rein on earth ever since Satan succeeded in wresting control of the planet from Adam. God does not always intervene to stop their malicious plans. He is allowing them to work their own plan here as an exhibit of what happens when beings rebel against Him. But God often does thwart them when they try to step beyond the bounds He has set.

Because their powers are essentially the same as nonrebellious angels, they can and often do impersonate messengers sent directly from God.

They want people to believe that evil spirits do not exist, or, failing that, to believe that all spirit beings are beneficent in nature.

They know just what people like and just how to best tempt people to follow them.

Although they always represent themselves as being on our side, their goal is to incite us to rebel against God, and then to accuse us of having initiated the rebellion in the hope that God will destroy us. In the end *they* will be destroyed.

Another limitation is self-imposed. They are opposed to God and truth, so it is in their nature to be deceptive. They find it difficult to tell the straight truth. They tend to tell a person exactly what he or she wants to hear.

That's the bad news.

The good news is that there are twice as many angels who did *not* rebel against God. They are opposite in character, yet just as mighty as the rebellious ones. They too can be contacted, but they delight to assist people in their battle against deception. They love to help people discover the truth.

The Bible records many instances in which loyal angels appeared to people, bringing messages from God and providing special help in response to their prayers.

When Jesus Christ was on earth, He had full authority to command the demon angels to leave His presence. Today we can still appeal in the name of Jesus to gain the victory over deceptive spirits.*

Is God Unfair?

Some people have accused God of being unfair for having allowed Satan to come to this planet and tempt people. But it would have been far more unfair if God had instead exercised the propaganda prerogative and simply denied that there was any choice of rulership in the universe. If He had refused Satan the right to present his case to Adam and Eve, He would have been just as unfair as any dictator today who throws his opponents into jail and denies the press the right to publish dissenting views.

Other people think God should simply have destroyed Satan at the outset of rebellion. Most dictators operate on that principle. Hitler was one. Khomeini is another. But God is too fair and wise to work that way. Suppressing rebellion by killing the rebels only postpones the inevitable overthrow of a government. It

84

leaves questions about the justice of the ruler. And where questions exist, rebellion will always crop up again and again until the government is overthrown.

The only effective way to destroy rebellion once and for all is to allow the rebels to have their way a limited time and place and then to let the subjects of the government decide whether the rebels' way is really better or not.

So God permitted Satan to live and to present his case for rebellion against God's government to Adam and Eve. But apparently Satan was not permitted to dog the footsteps of the newly created couple in his attempts to spread the rebellion to our planet. He seems to have had to limit his presence on earth to the vicinity of one tree in the middle of the Garden of Eden.

God warned Adam and Eve of Satan's presence. And He presented them with one simple way to demonstrate their continuing loyalty to Him. He told them not to eat the fruit of that tree at the center of the garden. He warned them that eating its fruit would constitute rebellion—joining forces with Satan—and would ultimately lead to their deaths.

Yet one day Eve found herself wandering near that tree. In a moment she was standing beside it, looking, wondering what could be so evil about it.

The First Channel

In that unguarded moment she heard a voice, and for the first time in history a human being began listening to a message from the second side of the spiritual realm.

What Eve saw and heard seemed to be a snake talking. It wasn't, however. The one whose voice she really heard was Satan, the liar and the father of lies.

He was simply using the snake as a channel for his message. That's why John the revelator refers to Satan as that "old serpent" (Revelation 12:9).

But his message was intriguing—enticing. It offered exactly what Eve wanted, just the way the entities who channel their messages today do.

The Bible records only two brief bursts of speech from that first channeled message: "Indeed, has God said, 'You shall not eat from any tree of the garden'?" (Genesis 3:1, NASB) and "You surely shall not die! For God knows that in the day you eat from it your eyes will be opened, and you will be like God, knowing good and evil" (verses 4, 5, NASB).

Those two brief utterances spoke a mouthful. The second assertion promised Eve the very thing that is still so enticing to people today: the opportunity to be their own God.

Altogether, those two sentences contain four important statements, or insinuations.

The first important implication is made silently, by insinuation: God is not truthful. He is not the ultimate source of truth. Indeed, it is impossible to know truth except by your own experience. You need the wisdom God has hidden from you to be able to discern what is really true. God knows, but He hasn't told you. You can't trust God.

The second important message is found in the outright lie "You surely shall not die." This statement implied more than simply that Eve would not fall down dead as soon as she ate the fruit. It declared that life is possible apart from the Creator who gives life. And that Eve was in and of herself immortal.

The third message grows out of the first two: You can improve your life, your enjoyment, your potential, by rebelling against God and doing things your own

way. You have infinite potential within yourself—
don't let anyone push you around and tell you what
you can and can't do. By ignoring God's rules, you can
unlock your full potential.

The fourth message is stated explicitly: "You will
be like God." Now, the first chapter of Genesis indi-
cates that God created human beings in His image,
after His likeness. But in chapter 3 the speaking
serpent seems to be addressing something more than
resemblance to God. He is stating what has become a
presupposition for the New Age movement. Divinity
lies within you. You are on a par with God. To achieve
your divine status, you need only assert your divinity
by rebelling against the One who claims to be God.

Take a moment right now to review these four
statements. Memorize them. And beware of them. If
you hear similar ideas coming from anyone today,
consider what the Bible says about their original
source. Satan no longer uses talking snakes. His
methods of deception have grown more sophisticated
through the years. The message is still the same,
though:

1. *God is not the source of truth.* There is no truth
except as you experience it (pluralism).

2. *You are immortal—you will not die.*

3. *You can fulfill your potential by separating yourself
from God.*

4. *You can be God yourself.*

Now let's jump for a moment from the first book of
the Bible to the last. Genesis tells of the creation of our
world and the beginning of the problems caused by
rebellion against God. The book of Revelation pictures
the final overthrow of the rebellion and the re-creation
of the world by God.

The Last Lie

It is important to note in Revelation 20 that Satan will continue to deceive people—using the same lies he did at the beginning—right up to his bitter end. Notice verses 7-9: "When the thousand years are over, Satan will be released from his prison and will go out to deceive the nations in the four corners of the earth—Gog and Magog—to gather them for battle. In number they are like the sand on the seashore. They marched across the breadth of the earth and surrounded the camp of God's people, the city he loves. But fire came down from heaven and devoured them" (NIV).

This scene takes place just before the final destruction of Satan and his followers—just before God completely re-creates the world for those who have maintained their faith in and loyalty to Him. They will inhabit this new earth for eternity. Notice the elements that are still implicit in Satan's deceptive rallying cry.

1. *God still is not the source of truth.* His proclamation that you must suffer eternal death is not true. Believe me (Satan) instead and we can beat Him.

2. *Follow me and you will not die.* We will defeat God and His people and take away their eternal city so we can live eternally there ourselves. You are immortal.

3. *You are separated from God, but that does not mean that you are powerless.* Indeed, your full potential is about to be achieved as we destroy those who have obeyed God and take away their city.

4. *You can usurp God's rulership by following me.* You can be God.

Thus, according to the Bible, Satan is the source of lies, and he will continue to perpetrate the very same deceptions until it has been clearly demonstrated to the universe that his rebellion against God has produced only evil and suffering. When that has been seen, it will at last be possible for God to destroy Satan and those who have rebelled with Him. No longer will the risk of having another rebellion erupt later lurk in the universe.

But until that time the deception goes on. And it is available to anyone who chooses not to accept God's rulership and the truth He has revealed in the Bible.

One of the strangest—and most terrifying—passages in all the Bible is 2 Thessalonians 2:1-12. This prophetic passage describes events that will take place before Jesus' second coming. It describes the antichrist, who works "in every sort of evil that deceives those who are perishing. They perish because they refused to love the truth and so be saved" (verse 10, NIV). And then Paul goes on to warn that God Himself will send upon these people who have failed to learn to love truth "a powerful delusion so that they will believe the lie" (verse 11, NIV).

Now, that sounds rather bad, admittedly, as if God Himself lies to people. But what's being described here is consistent with God's decision to allow Satan to come here and present his lies in the first place. God gives truth. But people who refuse to accept it have to be allowed to believe something. And the only choice other than truth is deception. God doesn't deceive people. But He does give people a free choice.

You Make the Choice

What it comes down to in the final analysis is that every person on earth has the opportunity either to believe the truth that God tells or to believe the lie that Satan tells. Those who fail to accept and cherish truth have no choice but to accept Satan's lies.

Everyone has the right to tap in to the power of

God and His loyal angels, or to tap in to the rebellion. Everyone has the right to choose truth—or deceit.

Accepting God's truth requires a response. It requires that we obey Him rather than disobey as Eve did when she chose the lie in place of the truth. But choosing to cooperate with God also unleashes all the power of God and His loyal angels to aid us in doing God's will.

Most people today show little or no interest in obeying God. They have set themselves up as their own god, and want to obey only their own will. We noted in chapter 5 that this is true particularly of those who have recently become channels.

But it is not only through the messages delivered by channels that Satan leads people to believe his lies today. After all, channels appeal only to a certain segment of society. But that doesn't matter to Satan. He is willing to present his deceptions however a person wants them.

After describing the beginning of Satan's rebellion in heaven, Revelation 12 goes on to describe his warfare against those who remain loyal to God. Revelation 13 predicts how the great climax of this warfare on earth will come about.

Satan's goal has always been to attract people to join his rebellion. In order to do that, he will, just before God puts an end to his rebellion, set up a situation similar to that in which Eve found herself back in Eden. It will be a situation in which people will have to make a decision between trusting God to provide their every need and trusting in themselves to sustain their lives.

Here's how Revelation 13 predicts that it will happen. The chapter describes a "beast" that Satan gives power to. In prophetic passages like this, beasts represent nations or rulers. This particular beast-nation sets up an either-or situation that affects the whole world. Revelation describes the situation in this way: "He also forced everyone, small and great, rich and poor, free and slave, to receive a mark on his right hand or on his forehead, so that no one could buy or sell unless he had the mark, which is the name of the beast or the number of his name" (Revelation 13:16, 17, NIV).

This either-or situation brings the question of rebellion against or trust in God to a head for the whole world. The question at stake for every individual is Will I accept the mark of the beast in order to maintain my right to buy and sell and pursue a livelihood and preserve my life, or will I refuse the mark of the beast and trust only in God to preserve my life?

Throughout the book of Revelation the mark of the beast is portrayed as the opposite of the seal of God, which represents total loyalty to and trust in God.

And the last verse of chapter 13 reveals just what is involved in receiving the mark or number of the beast: "This calls for wisdom. If anyone has insight, let him calculate the number of the beast, for it is man's number. His number is 666" (verse 18, NIV).

Stuck on 6

Through the years students of Scripture have applied this number to various specific individuals or powers. I will address some of these specifics in a later chapter. But for now it is important to note only the broad scope of what this number applies to. The Revised Standard Version states that this "is a *human* number" (emphasis supplied). Its rendering and that of the NIV are quite literal. The significance of the number is its human quality. This is the point that one gets from a literal reading of the Greek.

To understand the importance of 666 being a human number, you must know something about biblical numerology. In the Bible the number 7 signifies perfection, or completeness. Genesis 1 says that God created the earth in *seven* days. At the end of that period this planet was complete and perfect. Ever after that in the Bible 7 represented completeness.

The same chapter also tells us that God created humans on the *sixth* day of Creation week. Hence the significance of the numeral 6 as a symbol of humanity.

But 6 is one short of 7—thus, it is just short of perfection. This means that humans, apart from God, are imperfect. The *seventh* day of Creation week was the day on which God rested and the day He asked all human beings to rest and spend with Him. The *seventh* day was the day on which humans found their completeness in God. Apart from God, humanity's number is only 6—imperfect. But with God, humanity's number becomes 7—perfect.

The number 666, then, represents all the frailty and incompleteness of humans apart from God. It represents humans in rebellion against God. It represents Adam and Eve hiding from God after they ate the fruit of the forbidden tree. It represents all those who will ultimately be destroyed with Satan because they have separated themselves from God, the life-giver who makes humans complete and perfect. It represents all those who think they are perfect in and of themselves apart from God.

Thus one can receive the number of the beast in any number of ways. You need not listen to the message of a channel. You need only join the rebellion against God and learn to trust only in yourself to make provision for your future.

It all comes down to a matter of whom you trust.

And that makes it pretty easy to get the number 666, really. Unfortunately, few people today really trust God. And if you don't trust God, the only other choices available are Satan, self, and other humans. Trusting any one of those alternates leads to reception of the number of the beast—the number 666—mankind's imperfect number.

And that is where the real danger lies in the New Age movement. Not that it will, as some Christian writers have posited, become a form of resurgent Nazism and destined to take over the world and attempt to exterminate Christians. No. The devil has become much more subtle today. He knows that all he needs to do is to get people to trust in themselves instead of God.

And that's what the New Age movement is all about. It calls people to trust in the supposed infinite potential of human beings. As Marilyn Ferguson put it in one of the premier books about the New Age movement: "Rich as we are—together—we can do anything. We have it within our power to make peace within our torn selves and with each other, to heal our homeland, the whole earth" (*The Aquarian Conspiracy*, p. 406).

But is this vision real? Human pride says yes. The channels say yes. But the Bible (not to mention the history of mankind's attempts in the past) says no. Apart from God, human beings are incomplete and cannot heal themselves or their planet. The Bible tells us that God plans to intervene to heal not only the planet but the people who trust Him.

Yes, it all comes down to a matter of whom you trust. God's Word, commonly called the Bible, has proved to be a trustworthy source of truth for millennia. Should we abandon it now just because some upstart channel says we should? Or just because it goes against our human pride?

The Key to Understanding

Once you see in the book of Revelation God's explanation of the spiritual battle that rages here on our planet, it helps you understand the reason channels with anti-Bible messages are multiplying today. It helps you understand why Satan would want to send messages like the ones the channels are delivering today. It helps you understand just which supernatural powers are revealing secrets to the channels. It helps you understand how the channels can make some accurate predictions, but also why they often miss. And it helps you understand why the channeling entities so often practice deception.

Satan and his rebellious cohorts lurk behind many of the supernatural manifestations we see today. These fallen angelic beings are powerful. And they are deceptive. We dare not trust them. We dare not even tread on their turf without special protection from the loyal angels.

In each of the strands of the New Age movement that we will look at in later chapters, we will see that Satan's plan is being worked out in both supernatural and natural ways. Those who are looking for the supernatural find it, but those who want only the more naturalistic, content to rely on human power, are welcome in the movement as well.

Discerning the Spirits

Before going on to look at other aspects of this Satanic deception, we must consider one additional question. Since there are both good and bad angel operatives active in our world and since there is a Holy

Spirit of God as well as the evil spirit of Satan, how can we tell the difference?

Must we assume that every supernatural event is caused by deceptive, rebellious angels? Must we assume that every voice that speaks to us during meditation is a tempting spirit?

No. The Bible provides the way to discern good spirits from evil ones. "Do not believe every spirit, but test the spirits to see whether they are from God, because many false prophets have gone out into the world. This is how you can recognize the Spirit of God: Every spirit that acknowledges that Jesus Christ has come in the flesh is from God, but every spirit that does not acknowledge Jesus is not from God. This is the spirit of the antichrist, which you have heard is coming and even now is already in the world" (1 John 4:1-3, NIV).

The test seems simple enough. But be warned: deceptive spirits have read their Bibles well. They know how to make it sound as though they confess Jesus even though they don't.

The deceptive spirits speak often about the Christ or Christ consciousness or the cosmic Christ in order to make it sound as if they are in harmony with Christianity. But they are speaking of a generalized Christ spirit, which they claim has been incarnated into various bodies throughout eternity. They are not confessing that the one and only Son of God has come in the flesh once and for all.

Many of the channeled spirits today claim that they themselves are the spirit that incarnated in Jesus of Nazareth. They insist that they are now communicating Jesus' message, but through different means. But when we compare their messages with what Jesus taught while on earth and what He inspired prophets and apostles to write in the Bible, it becomes clear that this claim is just another of their habitual deceptions. Even a comparison of their messages to one another reveals contradictions and confusion.

We can be safe from deception by these spirits only when we rely on the revelations from the Holy Spirit that appear in the Bible. Every message, every supernatural manifestation, can be taken to this reference manual for comparison with the authentic message of God.

If the spirits, or inner voices, that speak to you confess that Jesus Christ has indeed come in the flesh as the unique Son of God, and if what they teach harmonizes with His teaching in the Bible, you can trust them.

---

*Information about Satan and his angels is derived from various passages throughout the Bible. Essential passages for understanding them and their mission include: Revelation 12; 13; 16:12-16; 20:1-10; Genesis 3:1-15; Job 1; 2:1-8; Ephesians 6:10-20; Isaiah 14:4-21, where Satan is described under the metaphor of the king of Babylon; and Ezekiel 28:11-19, where the metaphor of the king of Tyre is used for him.

Further passages that describe the work, nature, and destiny of Satan and his angels include: Zechariah 3:1-5; Matthew 4:1-11; 13:1-9, 36-43; Mark 1:21-28; 3:13-27; Luke 10:17, 18; 13:10-16; John 3:42-44; Acts 5:3; 26:15-18; 2 Corinthians 2:11; 11:1-15; 12:7; 2 Thessalonians 2:9; Hebrews 2:14; 1 Peter 5:8; 1 John 3:8-12; 5:18, 19; Jude 6-9; Matthew 25:41.

The following passages about nonrebellious angels shed light on the ways they can help people, and their activities in the struggle that is going on in the invisible world of spirits all around us: Genesis 19:1-22; 24:7; Exodus 3:2; 14:19; 23:20; Numbers 22:21-35; Judges 13:2-20; 2 Kings 19:35; Psalm 8:5; 34:7; 68:17; 91:11; 103:20; 104:4; Isaiah 63:9; Daniel 3:28; 6:22; Zechariah 4:1, 2; Matthew 1:20; 16:27; 18:10; 24:31-36; 26:53; 28:2; Mark 1:13; Luke 1:11-38; 2:9-16; 15:10; 20:36; 22:43; Acts 5:17-19; 8:26; 10:1-8; 12:6-11; 27:23; 2 Corinthians 11:13-15; 1 Timothy 5:21; Hebrews 2:9, 16; 12:22; 1 Peter 3:22; Jude 6, 7; Revelation 5:11; 10:1; 18:1; 21:12; 22:6-9.

CHAPTER

8

Is the New Age Something to Fear?

The strongest reaction to the New Age movement today comes from fundamentalist Christians, and rightly so. Hope for the New Age brought in by human effort or by evolving to a higher level cannot jibe with hope for the second coming of Jesus Christ.

But some Christian authors have set out to persuade the world that the movement consummates a longstanding conspiracy to take over the world, wipe out traditional religions, and establish a new society ruled by the antichrist. Is this what Christianity really has to fear from the New Age movement? Or is its threat more subtle?

One of the most widely read Christian books espousing the conspiracy view is Constance Cumbey's *Hidden Dangers of the Rainbow*. Cumbey believes that the New Age movement "truly meets the scriptural requirements for the antichrist and the political movement that will bring him on the world scene" (p. 39). Chapter 8, "The New Age Movement—The Fourth Reich?" sets out to prove the close parallel between the movement and Nazism. It attempts to show that the movement's leaders hope to succeed where Hitler failed. Cumbey believes that New Age leaders are planning to use force to take over the world.

Dave Hunt has brandished his quill against the movement in three major books. In the first, *Peace, Prosperity, and the Coming Holocaust* (subtitled *The New Age Movement in Prophecy*), he also shows the similarities between the movement and Nazism. He then goes on to speculate about how the leaders of the movement will take over the world after all the Christians have been raptured. In two more recent books Hunt turns his attention to marshaling evidence that the movement's philosophy has infiltrated the Christian church and is being taught from popular pulpits every week.

Texe Marrs, author of *Dark Secrets of the New Age* and *Mystery Mark of the New Age*, asserts that the movement's conspiratorial leaders believe that the New Age can only be brought in "after the earth has been fully cleansed of negative forces—such as traditional Christianity." Yet he admits that he can't really prove that this is what they would like to do. "It would," he writes, "be difficult—perhaps impossible—for us to gain access to the actual documents that reveal outright a hideous, hidden intent to persecute, purge, or kill all the Bible-believing Christians at some point in the future after the antichrist ascends to dictatorial power" (*Dark Secrets of the New Age*, pp. 136, 137).

In his second book on the topic Marrs asks: "Death, pain, bloodletting, chaos. Is this what lies just ahead for humanity? Is chaos and mass suffering inevitable to bring in a New Age of love, peace, and joy? The answer, according to the leaders of the New Age, is yes, this is what it will take for mankind to become godkind" (*Mystery Mark of the New Age*, p. 153). A series of quotations from various New Age sources, which describe the kind of chaos that must ensue before the tranquillity of the New Age can commence, follows this introduction to the chapter "Marked for Extinction: A Death Sentence for Christians."

If we accept the alarm these authors are sounding, then everyone in the world, not just Christians, has some rather rough times to look forward to. And the troubles will come courtesy of New Age leaders who are trying to take over the world.

Do we have something to fear from the New Age movement? Is it resurgent Nazism? Will its dictatorial leaders plunge the world into chaos worse even than that which Hitler brought upon us?

Or is the movement merely, as Marilyn Ferguson described it, a "benign conspiracy for a new human agenda"? (*The Aquarian Conspiracy*, p. 23).

My own research into this question has not turned up any reliable evidence of a movement with strong similarity—on the human level—to the Nazi Party in Germany during the period between the two world wars. The Nazi Party was a tight-knit, hierarchically structured organization with a strong central leader who consolidated his power through propaganda and violence, along with involvement in the occult.

The New Age movement's chief similarity to Nazism lies in its involvement with the occult, which is indeed sufficient cause for concern. But a single leader has not yet emerged who can bring together all the diverse factions within the movement.

And as we noted in chapter 6 not even the various channels can agree among themselves whether the New Age will come in peacefully or through violence.

At this point the occult connection yields contradictory messages because Lucifer is willing to tell people exactly what they want to hear.

How to Find a Conspiracy

A researcher who sets out to find evidence of a pattern or conspiracy in the writings of New Age authors can find it. But at the same time, this person must ignore the evidences that the movement is still a highly diverse, loosely knit network.

Both Marrs and Cumbey set out to prove a close-knit conspiracy that is just biding its time, waiting for an opportunity to exterminate Christians. But to prove this point they have to misuse their sources.

For example, when trying to prove that New Age leaders favor exterminating Christians, Marrs quotes from New Age sources that predict destruction which will come about as a result of *natural* catastrophes (such as Ruth Montgomery's long-predicted shift of the earth on its axis). But Marrs makes it appear as though the New Age writer is describing what he or she thinks New Age *people* will have to do to get rid of Christians.

Cumbey cites a passage in which a New Age writer describes a natural separation he expects to come about between New Age enlightened spirits and other spirits. But Cumbey makes it appear as though the New Age author advocates human intervention to rid earth of all who are not ready for the New Age to dawn.

In addition, both authors find their best material by consulting the most radical of New Age authors and quoting them as representative of the entire movement. Such an approach is analogous to an anti-Christian author quoting Jim Jones's suicide appeal to his Jonestown commune as a representative sample of current Christian preaching.

Hunt, on the other hand, confines himself to speculative interpretation of prophecy. He makes room for the New Age conspiracy to take over the world after Jesus comes back and raptures all the Christians, who then won't be available to be killed by the New Age antichrist.

Although I also view the movement from a Christian perspective, Cumbey and Marrs have lost credibility with me by their misuse of sources. And I can't buy Hunt's prophetic speculations.

Which is not to say that I see nothing to fear in the New Age movement. While it may not be a close-knit organization on the human level, in my reading I have turned up strong evidence that there is organization at the superhuman level that is working to knit together the network of people who are listening to the various spirits that proclaim the imminence of the New Age.

High-Level Organization

Back in the 1960s, when the spirits were laying the groundwork for the New Age movement as we know it today, they sent messages about the New Age through the spiritualist medium Arthur Ford. The entity who spoke through Ford while Ford was in a trance called himself Fletcher.

When Fletcher addressed himself to the issue of the coming New Age, he made a special point of telling where and to whom we should look for the illumination that would bring in this age of enlightenment. In chapter 3 I mentioned that Fletcher said the enlightenment must come from the East. But he became more specific than that when people questioned him.

And therein lies a most interesting and intriguing story. It shows the interconnectedness of the New Age movement on the spirit level.

On November 2, 1964, Ford held a sitting for a man from England by the name of Anthony Brooke. In that sitting Fletcher related a story from one of his friends in the spirit world. His friend had met and talked with Sun Myung Moon, Korean founder of the Unification Church. Moon teaches that the New Age began in 1960 and that he is the Messiah of the New Age.

In 1964 the spirits, speaking through Ford, testified to the fact that Moon was indeed "a teacher, a revealer"—"the voice of this Intelligence—Creative Mind—which you call God" (*Unknown but Known*, p. 119).

Now, it might seem at first glance that this testimony has nothing to do with the New Age movement as we know it today. Moon and his church are far out on the fringe of the movement, if they are even to be included at all. None of the recent (1980s) New Age or anti-New Age writings that I have read even mentions Moon as part of the movement. He seems to have fallen out of favor with the mainstream.

But the apparent separation between Moon and the rest of the New Age movement is only on the surface. Beneath the surface, at the level on which the movement is being organized and promoted by deceptive spirits, Moon's group can be considered very much a part of the New Age framework. It is part of the broad-spectrum deception that they are spreading all over the world. This fact became apparent when Anthony Brooke asked Fletcher about the relationship between Moon and "the spirit that is appearing in England that calls himself Truth."

"That's Mr. Moon's projection—a form of apparition—the projection of the Spirit of Truth—who expresses himself through Mr. Moon," Fletcher replied (*ibid.*, p. 122). That connection to the spirit called Truth in England is the evidence that Moon is linked at the spirit level to the mainstream of the New Age movement. For when David Spangler joined the Findhorn Community in Scotland in 1970, the transmissions he received, which form the basis for his book *Revelation: The Birth of a New Age,* came from the same spirit that had earlier revealed itself under the name Truth in England. (Spangler explains the connection of the spirit that spoke to him with this earlier Truth on pages 42 and 43. See also Anthony Brooke, *Revelation for the New Age*, pp. 62, 64.) Thus Findhorn's guiding spirit of the New Age has been identified, at the spirit level, as Sun Myung Moon!

It is possible (but hardly probable) that Spangler and Brooke never made the connection between Spangler's spirit mentor and Moon. But at the level on which the New Age movement is being organized the connection is well-known.

And though the messages that have come through Fletcher/Ford, Moon, and Spangler are not identical, their import in relation to the part of Jesus, Christianity, and the Second Coming in bringing in the New Age is identical. To Lucifer it does not matter which of them we believe.

"The Jesus of Galilee will not return," Fletcher told a group of Koreans, including Moon, on March 18, 1965. "It is not necessary. The Christ who manifested through him is the Eternal—He will manifest again. He has never ceased to speak to men but the time has come when, in the New Age, the veil which has been drawn between your plane and the World of Spirit will be pushed aside and those who have been freed from physical bondage will be able to speak and use and guide and teach the peoples of earth. That is being brought into manifestation everywhere.

"But the important thing to remember is that when God wants to make a revelation (He has always done so and always will) He has to choose a human instrument, who, through some circumstances or conditions, has been brought to the point of sensitiveness and spiritual perception so that *he* can, in his own person, accept this ancient light of wisdom—and through him it will filter down to others. . . .

"There come periodically in the history of the race moments when the Holy Spirit has to individualize almost completely in some person—who becomes the instrument who will enable others to catch the Spirit and see the Spirit, and know the Spirit. . . .

"Sun Myung Moon is the one I have been talking about" (Ford, pp. 126, 127).

Moon is willing to accept this role as the Lord of the Second Coming, thus making the return of Jesus unnecessary. (Although Moon may be reluctant to claim this title openly, Ronald Enroth, in *The Lure of the Cults and New Religions*, pp. 81, 82, points out that Moon's followers are neither reluctant to attribute nor dissuaded from attributing it to him.)

As for the spirit who spoke to Spangler, calling itself Limitless Love and Truth, its message is that there need not be a second coming of Christ, because LL&T is itself the I AM of all creation and is creating the New Age world even now in our midst (*Revelation: The Birth of a New Age*, pp. 84ff.).

So do we have something to fear from the New Age movement? Yes! We must fear deception. We must fear that it is founded on messages from the same spirit that deceived Eve in Eden. And we must fear that this spirit will work in secret, behind the scenes, insidiously destroying faith in the Bible as the word of God.

We must fear that those Christians who are watching on the walls, preparing to meet a frontal assault from New Age leaders, will find themselves fortified within an easily outflanked spiritual Maginot Line.

The Christian Maginot Line

Before World War II began, the French military establishment spent millions of francs fortifying the Maginot Line, a series of fortifications along the border between France and Germany, to withstand an enemy whose tactics they thought they understood. They *knew* that if Hitler marched against France, he would not—could not—come through the low countries. He would have to throw the weight of his forces against the massive fortifications of the Maginot.

And the French Army prepared for his attack. Miles of barbed wire, tank traps, and machine gun emplacements protected the eastern side of the line. Massed cannon bristled from its bunkers. A complex communication and tunnel system made it possible to reinforce whichever part of the line might come under attack without exposing troop movements to view or bombardment.

But when fighting on Germany's western front began, the troops holed up inside the Maginot fortifications soon found themselves surrounded by the German *Wermacht*, which had pushed its way through the weakly defended low countries. The Maginot guns could not even be turned to face the direction from which the enemy finally came!

The same thing can happen if we Christians concentrate only on conspiracy theories in anticipation of a frontal assault upon our churches. Worse yet, viewing New Age people as conspirators with a secret plan to wipe out Christianity creates an atmosphere of alienation between Christians and the many people who are seeking spiritual enlightenment.

In reality, New Age enthusiasts are, by and large, people much like the people we meet in our churches from week to week. They are spiritual seekers. They are people who want to cooperate to make the future better. They don't have horns or pointed tails, and they don't build torture racks in their basements and come together to discuss what fun it is going to be to torture Christians and force them to abandon their faith.

Many have been deeply wounded by Christians, or have become disillusioned with churches that seem more interested in self-preservation than in doing something to improve the world.

In their hurt and disillusionment they have gone seeking better ways to bring about cooperation, peace, and improvement for our world.

In their seeking, many have fallen for the deceptively optimistic New Age lie that evil spirits are propagating these days. But these people are not beyond hope. They are not beyond our help. We must not hole ourselves up in our churches, fortifying ourselves against them.

They have needs just as we do. Needs that can only be truly met and fulfilled in Jesus Christ.

In the following chapters we will examine how these people are reaching out for help, expressing needs that we can help them find fulfillment for. We will look at the New Age-oriented solutions they are finding, and will examine how we can help them find better solutions.

CHAPTER
9

Holistic Health

The only kind of crystal most Americans used to own was the kind that fancy goblets are made from. But that's all changing as people have started tuning in to the New Age movement.

Recently I attended what was billed as an ESP psychic fair in Bethesda, Maryland, just outside the District of Columbia and only a mile or so from the front entrance of the National Institutes of Health. I attended because I wanted to see if there was any tie-in between the psychics operating there and the New Age movement. I also wanted to see what kind of people patronize psychics these days.

The answer to my first question was yes. Among the people offering psychic consultations were some who made it a point to use the phrase *New Age* in connection with their work. The answer to my second question was: all kinds. A wide variety of people crowded into the meeting room, which had about 30 tables set up for various psychics to practice their trade.

I spoke briefly with a number of psychics and with several of their customers. A professional-appearing man in his 20s told me he had stopped by out of curiosity, but after sitting down and conversing with a psychic, he was favorably impressed by her noncommercial attitude. He was seriously considering going back and paying her to do a reading for him.

A middle-aged lady told me I really should get a reading from one of the psychics. She couldn't tell me for sure just why, but she felt that I should. "After all, what's $20?" she asked. It would be worth a try. But a retired lady told me that this was not the best place to get a reading. She suggested that I go to Florida, where there is an entire city of psychics. There I could get a reading in a much more private setting.

One of the psychics, a man in his late 20s, told me that when he meditates he sees a little creature that looks like the epitome of wisdom. It materializes in front of him and whispers to him.

A young woman told me that by looking carefully at a person she could see his or her aura and could detect which parts of the body were not functioning up to full potential.

I heard an older woman who looked like a traditional gypsy fortuneteller instruct a young woman to go outside at night, look up at the stars, and invite the "Space Brothers" to speak to her.

People of all ages and classes listened intently to the messages of psychics and healers, seeking some key to make their lives better.

Among the arts practiced at the fair were tarot, palmistry, I-Ching, physiognomy, psychic healing, life readings, astrology, aura readings, aura painting, Mah-Jongg, past-life regression, and New Age portrait painting, which is designed to help a person become aware of his or her higher self.

How to Recharge

But by far the busiest corner of the room was the one occupied by a large middle-aged lady who had set up a display of various crystals, stones, and seashells, along with a few bottles of Edgar Cayce massage oil. An assemblage of customers kept her busy answering questions and making sales. I peered at her wares as she waved her hand across her display of small stones—agates, Apache tears, and other polished pebbles. "I keep a bunch of these in the bottom of my purse all the time," she told a customer. "Then when I'm up against a hard situation, I can just reach in and feel around till I get the right one and hold it for a while to kind of recharge."

What kind of charge was she getting out of rocks? You might well ask such a question if you haven't been in contact with this particular side of the New Age movement.

A New Age catalog I have in my file offers a pouch containing "10 of the world's most beautiful, energized stones from nature's mineral kingdom. Carry them with you; hold one or two while meditating —allow the energy of these stones to aid your mental, emotional, and physical well-being." The same page of the catalog explains the value of Apache tears, which are little bits of obsidian: "Mysterious obsidian, the stone of transformation and mastery over the physical plane. . . . A favorite with healers and metaphysicians, obsidian is a magnetically beautiful stone" (*Pyramid Books and the New-Age Collection*, p. 5).

But these bits of gravel are not the favorites of New Age stone merchants. To them, crystals are the real source of power (and money). "Clear quartz crystal," an insert to the same catalog asserts, "attracts and transmits energy, can penetrate from one dimension of existence into another. Use for healing, aura-balancing, transformation.

"Rose quartz," on the other hand, the catalog says, "is a strong healer of the heart. Its soft, gentle color promotes the ideal of universal love." And: "Amethyst [purple quartz] is a stone of power, protection, peace, and spirituality. Relates to the Crown Chakra, gateway to higher forces."

Crystals are important in the work of some New Age holistic healers. "Practicing crystal healing is an opportunity to let go and let God," writes Katrina Raphaell in a statement that sounds almost like it is based on the Christian principle of trust in the God revealed in the Bible. But in the next sentence she explains which god she is referring to: "It is the time when the heart listens to the messages of the soul, a time to plunge deeply into trust in the inner self" (*Crystal Healing, Vol. 2—The Therapeutic Application of Crystals and Stones,* cited in *The New Age Catalogue,* p. 22). The only god she connects with crystal healing is the god of self—the god of the imperfect number 666 instead of the Creator who truly wants to heal us and raise us to the level of perfection.

But crystal healing is just one small branch of the large field of holistic health that has become attached to the New Age movement. New Age-oriented people are looking for better ways to total health.

The Whole Person

There is certainly nothing wrong with the concept of holism (or wholism, as some spell it) in health. The idea behind it is that we should treat the whole person in trying to make him or her well, rather than just trying to alleviate specific symptoms. This concept comes somewhat as a revolution in Western medicine. The empirical methodology of the laboratory has become so central that a patient often has to visit a series of specialists, each one dealing with one aspect of his or her therapy, while leaving all other aspects to the care of other specialists.

The problem that arises with holistic health is one that stems from the human tendency to overreact, to "throw the baby out with the bathwater." And not only that, to "let the fox in with the hens." In their reaction against Western medicine, with its array of chemicals, drugs, and potions for every ailment, many people jettison the good with the bad. In their search for better ways some people have become willing to experiment with any form of medicine that doesn't come with a pharmaceutical company's name on the label. Because some people seem to equate Western medicine with evil, they have lost the ability to discern the good and bad in other forms of medicine.

Mystical Medicine

As a result, many strange and mystical ideas have become associated with New Age holistic medicine. Edgar Cayce was probably the one man who did more to bring mysticism to the holistic healing field than anyone else. Although he died in 1945, his influence on some of the people connected with the New Age movement and holistic medicine is extremely powerful to this day.

Cayce was a psychic and a spiritual healer. While in a trance he would prescribe cures for various illnesses. The cures often worked, but not for any scientifically credible reasons. His work was in many ways similar to that of a traditional shaman.

It is not surprising that the messages channeled through him while he was in a trance state were identical in philosophy to those we hear from channels today. He taught reincarnation, monism, and other Eastern metaphysical concepts—and pointed to the year 1998 for the dawning of the New Age (Mary Ellen Carter, *Edgar Cayce on Prophecy*, p. 29).

Fritjof Capra, a physicist and leading New Age thinker, demonstrates another connection between holism and New Age thought in *The Turning Point*, which is published under Bantam Books' New Age label: "To develop a holistic approach to health . . . , we do not need to break completely fresh ground but can learn from medical models existing in other cultures. Modern scientific thought . . . is leading to a view of reality that comes very close to the views of mystics and of many traditional cultures, in which knowledge of the human mind and body and the practice of healing are integral parts of natural philosophy and of spiritual discipline" (p. 305).

In explaining what he means by this, he points out that "in nonliterate cultures throughout the world, the origin of illness and the process of healing have been associated with forces belonging to the spirit world, and a great variety of healing rituals and practices have been developed to deal with illness accordingly. Among these, the phenomenon of shamanism offers a number of parallels to modern psychotherapies" (*ibid.*, p. 306). The aim of shamanistic healing, he writes, "is to reintegrate the patient's condition into the cosmic order" (*ibid.*, p. 308).

Capra, a physicist, wanders from his field of expertise when he writes about medicine and healing. But he believes an experience in 1970 qualifies him to speak in matters related to the spirit world. While meditating one day, he suddenly became aware of "the atoms of the elements and those of my body participating in [the] cosmic dance of energy; I felt its rhythm and I 'heard' its sound, and at that moment I *knew* that this was the dance of Shiva, the lord of dancers worshiped by the Hindus" (*The Tao of Physics*, p. xix). That moment yielded the inspiration that led to his book *The Tao of Physics*, in which he attempts to demonstrate that the most recent discoveries of theoretical physicists confirm that the ancient Hindu and Buddhist sages were right all along about the illusory nature of reality and the oneness of all things.

Capra's thesis is typical New Age. It springs from a desire to find within his own humanity, and through contact with the spirit world, the solution to the multitude of problems that face our world. This desire leads naturally to a connection with Eastern religion rather than with Christianity, because the Eastern focus is inward (to find the god within) rather than outward (toward a God outside of humanity), as in Christianity, Judaism, and Islam.

Crystal Healing

A multitude of therapies flourishes under the heading of holistic health. Crystal healing is only a small part, but it serves as a good example because it draws on all aspects the holistic vision of health.

It is connected to nature—using natural objects rather than medicines and treatments concocted by modern science. Edgar Cayce taught that millennia ago the inhabitants of the now-lost continent Atlantis used a "great crystal" to rejuvenate their bodies so they could live for hundreds of years (Carter, p. 55).

It relates to vibrational levels. Much of New Age theory is built around vibrations. Most New Age channels agree that the New Age will be brought to fruition when the earth shifts to a higher vibrational level.

It relates to the Eastern concept of *chakras*. Hinduism teaches that the human body has seven chakras, or centers of energy. The lowest level of energy is at the base of the spine, which vibrates in the red light frequency range. The progression ends at the crown of the head, whose chakra vibrates in the violet range. Various types of crystals are supposed to resonate with different chakras.

Through their connection with the chakras, crystals also become associated with the concept of Ch'i, the universal, invisible life energy that, Eastern philosophy teaches, flows through the 12 meridians of the body.

All these concepts are associated also with various other therapies and techniques that are included under the heading of holistic health. These include aura reading, which is done by people who claim to be able to sense which of the chakras may be blocked or not functioning to their full potential; acupuncture, acupressure, and therapeutic touch, which are said to work because of their ability to influence the flow of the Ch'i through the meridians; and even chiropractic, which was based originally on the theory that adjusting the spine can facilitate the transmission of energy from the spinal cord to other parts of the body.

Crystal healing is also closely related to shamanism, because crystals can be viewed as power objects that impart magical abilities to their possessor. Carlos Castaneda, whose descriptions of the work of a Mexican Indian shaman are popular New Age reading, deals extensively with the use of power objects.

American Indian shamanism seems to be quite

popular in some New Age circles, judging from the sundry advertisements for Medicine Wheel Gatherings with medicine man Sun Bear that I find in New Age publications. Medicine Wheel Gatherings include ceremonies for healing not only people but the whole earth. Cooperating with Sun Bear in these gatherings is Ngakpa Chogyam, a tantric shaman from Tibet.

While there may be nothing wrong with or harmful in most holistic therapies and techniques, involvement with them tends to lead down the road to involvement with the occult. You see, acceptance of Eastern and shamanistic techniques prepares a person to accept Eastern metaphysics as well, especially the concept of Brahman, which is the basis of much holistic teaching today.

According to Hindu teaching, "Brahman, the non-personal Supreme One, pervades all things and transcends all things. Of this great principle, the Rig Veda states, 'Though men call it by many names, it is really One.' An essential part of the teaching regarding Brahman is the belief that man can, by personal effort, and use of inner knowledge, attain union with this Divine One while still on earth" (Ross, *Three Ways of Asian Wisdom*, p. 19). Another term used to describe this concept is *monism*.

Monism is the foundation of psychic healing as practiced by healers such as Olga Worral. Although Worral professes a strong belief in God, and does healings in a Methodist church in Baltimore, she teaches that "spiritual healing occurs when a therapist becomes enough in tune with both the universal mind and the patient to become a channel of energy from one to the other" (Paul C. Reisser, M.D., Teri K. Reisser, and John Weldon, *New Age Medicine*, p. 103). In her contact with the universal mind, Worral has had many experiences with spirit beings.

The Meditation Connection

Connection with the occult is especially strong in techniques that involve meditation.

In 1959 Maharishi Mahesh Yogi introduced transcendental meditation (TM) to the United States, and over the next decade hundreds of thousands of people learned the technique. Then in 1970 Dr. Robert Keith Wallace began researching the effects of TM and found that it yielded extremely beneficial results through relaxation and reduction of stress.

TM is billed as a way to reap the benefits of meditation that Hindu and Buddhist monks have enjoyed through the years without having to accept any religious doctrines. What the person learning TM may or may not be told, though, is that the mantra that must be repeated to enter the meditative state is always a "primal word" from the Upanishads, the ancient Hindu scriptures. A favorite word among New Age meditators is *Om*, which is said to be the single sound that was present at the foundation of the universe, and so is said to have tremendous creative power.

If you remember the Harmonic Convergence of August 15, 1987, you may remember the bemusement that many reporters expressed in describing New Age people gathering to hold hands and hum at spiritual centers all around the world. But the sound that arose from the harmonic gatherings was not humming—it was a collective utterance of that supposedly powerful word *Om*—uttered in unison in hope that enough people meditating and saying it at the same time could focus creative power and help to raise the vibrational level of the world and avert disaster.

Religious indoctrination may not be part of TM training. Nonetheless, the TM technique in itself can be dangerous if during meditation the meditator learns to turn off the rational part of his or her mind. This could open up the deeper levels of consciousness to contact with spirit guides who might be waiting for just such a chance to lead the meditator down the path of deception.

An Idle Mind

The old saying "An idle mind is the devil's workshop" contains more truth than most people realize. Any form of meditation that calls for shutting off the active thinking and discerning processes automatically opens the door to influence by supernatural spirits.

When Arthur Ford instructed Ruth Montgomery on how to begin automatic writing, he told her first of all to enter meditation, then to pick up a pencil and hold it on a blank sheet of paper. It was while she was in this meditative state that "an unseen force seemed to seize her hand and guide the pencil in circles and figure eights, around and around and around. 'I was puzzled,' she admits. 'This was supposed to convey messages, not circles, but I knew I had not knowingly propelled the pencil.'

"An hour later she called on a colleague who was also interested in the psychic. 'Oh, Ruth,' the friend exclaimed, 'I've just received a message through automatic writing that says "Now Ruth can do this." ' " Ruth then showed the friend the piece of paper with circles and figure eights drawn on it, and her friend assured her that such figures were the way that automatic writing always begins (Ruth Montgomery with Joanne Garland, *Ruth Montgomery: Herald of the New Age*, pp. 97, 98).

From the contact with the friend it became obvious that what was happening to Ruth was not simply a product of her own mind. While in the meditative trance, she had contacted a spirit outside herself who was able to contact and communicate with others as well.

Meredith Lady Young, author of *Agartha*, describes the way she first came into contact with her spirit guide, called Mentor: "With my legs folded yoga-style, hands resting lightly on my knees, I began doing my deep breathing. Closing my eyes, I silently voiced my personal affirmation which preceded each meditation: 'I believe that I am more than my physical body and as such can perceive more than my physical world. I ask that I be assisted in my search for truth by whatever means is appropriate to advancing my ultimate awareness.' . . .

"Slowly I counted myself into deeper levels of meditation, letting the strands of quiet merge inside me. . . . I allowed myself the luxury of totally letting go and found my mind drifting on magical inner currents. Then, at a point deep in meditation, I shifted my body position, bringing my hands lightly together in my lap. The effect was dramatic. As my fingers touched, an electrical impulse jammed my entire being, and a circle of intense energy began to circulate in a counterclockwise motion through my hands, up my left arm, through my head, and back down my right arm." Soon she picked up the notepad and pencil she always kept at her side during meditation, and her hand began to draw circles. Later when her hand started writing, the first automatic writing session filled 47 pages (*Agartha*, pp. 25, 26).

Of the channels and psychics I have studied, nearly every one first came in contact with his or her spirit guide while practicing some form of Eastern meditation. Shamans also typically use a chant or mantra to achieve the trance state in which they make contact with the spirit world.

As to the nature of the spirits that contact people during meditation, even Ruth Montgomery cautions that "once we have raised our vibrations sufficiently to contact the spirit plane while in the alpha state, it is as easy for an evil entity to reach us as it is for a benign one" (*Threshold to Tomorrow*, p. 256).

There is a type of meditation that is safe for Christians to practice, but it does not involve any technique for emptying the mind. Rather it involves filling the mind with the words of the Bible, then seeking the Holy Spirit's guidance as you thoughtfully ponder and seek to mine the depths of the passage for spiritual insight.

Affirmations and Visualization

Perhaps you noticed a second important element in Meredith Lady Young's approach to the spirit world. It comes under various titles, typically *affirmation* or *positive visualization*. It is also a widely accepted part of the holistic health movement because it brings together the efforts of body and mind to enable healing.

Its basis is found in the theories espoused by spirit entities such as Seth, who channeled through Jane Roberts. Seth counseled one husband, whose wife was dying with multiple sclerosis, that "he should imagine the energy and vitality of the universe filling his wife's form with health. . . . If possible, he should touch her during this exercise, and it should be done morning, evening, and night." Furthermore, Seth said, the wife should go to a hypnotist who could "instill positive suggestions to rouse her will to live" (*The Seth Material*, pp. 149, 150).

Certainly there is nothing wrong with positive thinking—many illnesses in the world are caused by negative thoughts. But Seth and other spirit entities carry the theory much further than just thinking good thoughts. They teach that everything in our world, be it good or bad, is the product of our own thoughts. Therefore, we can change our reality simply by changing our thoughts and choosing a different reality.

In the case of the woman with multiple sclerosis, though, Seth explained, simply changing her thoughts at this time would not work a cure because the disease was the result of a choice her spirit had made prior to taking up residence in its present body. Her choice to be crippled resulted from the fact that in a previous life she had lived as an Italian man who had resented his crippled daughter. Now in this life she was simply working out her *karma* (a Hindu term that describes how we reap the fruits of our present and past actions either in this life or in future incarnations) by taking the role of a crippled person (*ibid.*, pp. 151, 152).

This is just one illustration of how the holistic health field links itself tightly to Eastern metaphysical ideas such as reincarnation. Because of this link, people who set out to discover a more healthy lifestyle these days are often quickly sucked into the world of Eastern meditation and spiritualism.

Human Potential

One way in which the holistic health aspect of the New Age movement is infiltrating our society with its ideas is through what is commonly called the "human potential movement." This movement's most obvious manifestation is in the motivation and success seminars that bring New Age ideas to businesses to help their employees become more productive.

In 1985 such a seminar was even brought, in video form, to the church organization that I work for. The New Age Thinking Seminar was advertised as "a dynamic video presentation of ideas and principles resulting in increased job satisfaction and productivity."

This kind of thinking is, of course, attractive to any employer. But according to a segment on the television program *20/20*, many employees are beginning to rebel against being compelled to attend such seminars. They are complaining that the instructors use religious indoctrination and try to change the students' worldview.

A training professional from one large corporation recently wrote to the *Training and Development Journal* and expressed fear that the training industry is "being used to proselytize New Age religion under the deceptive marketing of increased productivity, self-actualization, and self-improvement" (cited by Richard Watring, "New Age Training in Business: Mind Control in Upper Management?" *Eternity*, February 1988, p. 30).

Also included in the human potential movement are drastic encounter therapy groups such as Werner Erhard's Forum (formerly EST) and John Hanley's Lifespring. Hundreds of thousands of people have attended these programs in which the leader uses a highly authoritarian and confrontational style to break down participants' normal thought patterns, thus forcing new ways of thinking. What the programs really do is foster a paradigm shift that leads to the New Age belief that everyone creates his or her own reality.

Once the participants have accepted that viewpoint, the next step is into positive visualization techniques for creating a better future. Hypnosis and meditation can play a large part in such exercises, and some leaders even encourage seminar attendees to use channeling as a means toward higher creativity (*ibid.*, p. 31).

Christians and Holism

Christians have no argument with the basic concept of treating illness from a whole-person standpoint. And there is much to be said for the value of positive thinking and a hope-filled lifestyle. But the devil is stealing a march on us by taking these good concepts and linking them to the belief that we can create our own world aided by messages from the spirit world.

Christianity has much to contribute to the holistic health field because the Scriptures reveal the workings of the Creator of human bodies.

The vegetarian diet that God gave Adam and Eve in the Garden of Eden is the ideal diet for human health and longevity. Scientific studies have shown that Seventh-day Adventists who follow a vegetarian lifestyle live an average of six years longer than people on a typical American diet. And they have fewer aches, pains, and diseases in old age as well.

When God created the first humans, He gave them physical work to do in tending their garden home six days a week. Research has validated the importance of physical exercise in maintaining good health. But God went a step further and also provided for people to have one day of rest every week. The Sabbath rest day can bring tremendous benefits to stressed-out people of our day.

TM may help people cope with stress and tension,

but trust in God goes beyond mere relaxation by helping people overcome anxiety by learning not to worry.

I have tried to fathom a few of the Edgar Cayce readings on how to attain and maintain health, but I have found them almost unintelligible. A much better source of good counsel on holistic health is to be found in the writings of Ellen G. White, a deeply committed Christian author who received much of what she learned about health in visions given by God. Her counsels are written out in plain, easily read English. She wrote on health topics from 1863 until her death in 1915, and doctors today testify that she was more than 100 years ahead of her time in her understanding of health.*

Rather than letting us create our own reality and suffer in later lives for all the sins and mistakes we commit in this life, God—who sees all and knows all—takes personal care of our destiny. And He provides grace and forgiveness so that we need not return here to live miserable lives again and again. The apostle John expressed God's will for us in 3 John 2: "I pray that you may enjoy good health and that all may go well with you" (NIV).

God wants us to take good care of our bodies. He calls them the temples of the Holy Spirit (1 Corinthians 6:19). So Christians have much in common with people who are interested in holistic health. As Christians we should be reaching out to them and showing them that they do not need to use the hocus-pocus remedies of the shaman. And they need not look only within for strength to overcome disease. We should introduce them to the God outside of them, who cares deeply for each one and who wants all to be in good health.

*Books by E. G. White on health and healing include: *Counsels on Health, Counsels on Diet and Foods, The Ministry of Healing,* and *Mind, Character, and Personality.* These books are readily available in inexpensive editions. The first two are published by Pacific Press Publishing Association, Box 7000, Boise, Idaho 83707 (800) 447-7377. The last two are published by the Review and Herald® Publishing Association, 55 West Oak Ridge Drive, Hagerstown, Maryland 21740 (800) 777-9098.

CHAPTER
10

Reincarnation

Belief in reincarnation lies at the roots of the currently popular New Age hope. To most believers the New Age would be both meaningless and unattainable without a belief in reincarnation.

First, because reincarnation provides the basis for the hope that human spirits have now evolved through many lifetimes to the point at which they can make the transition to a higher level of consciousness. Some writers describe this as a new stage of evolution in which humanity will advance from its current status as *Homo sapiens* to the higher, wiser level of *Homo noeticus* or *Homo universalis*.

Second, because the journey of the soul, or spirit, to a nonphysical realm after death is the basis for belief in the channeling of messages from this higher realm. Such messages typically purport to be from a more highly evolved being who has either gone on from this planet or has never lived here. Other New Age teachers say that the messages come from a person's own "higher self," in which there is awareness of the things the spirit has learned through various incarnations.

Third, because belief in reincarnation assures everyone of a chance to participate in and enjoy the benefits of the New Age. It allows a person to believe that no matter how badly things may go in this life, he or she will have a chance to come back again in the New Age when things will be better.

Fourth, because reincarnation provides a system of justice that does away with the need of a savior and a god who will judge people. It allows people to atone for their own sins by coming back in a new life and working through the things they failed to overcome in the previous life.

For these reasons, belief in reincarnation serves both as a stimulus to lead people to believe in the coming New Age and as a sustainer of the New Age hope.

It should be noted, though, that the reincarnation belief adopted by Western New Age devotees bears only moderate relationship to the belief of either Hindus or Buddhists.

Hinduism teaches that when a person dies, the soul will sooner or later incarnate as another creature—human, animal, or plant. This is, incidentally, called *transmigration*, not reincarnation. The goal of the multiplied lifetimes of an individual is to reunite with Brahman—the timeless, formless everything from which individual souls have become separated because of an imbalance in the universe. Once a person becomes one with Brahman, transmigrations cease and suffering comes to an end.

According to Buddhist teachings, the conscious soul does not survive death (a belief that, if accepted, would wreak havoc with New Age belief), but somehow the flame of life does at some point become rekindled in another being after death. The goal of reincarnation for the Buddhist is to rid oneself of all desire, thus achieving *nirvana* and ceasing to incarnate and suffer.

The typical New Age teaching about reincarnation sees the individual at death simply as passing from one realm of consciousness into another, perhaps to live on another planet or just on another vibrational level for a time. Then, if necessary, the individual may decide to come back to earth to live another life and work toward perfection. The goal of all this is never expressed in Hindu or Buddhist terms, though. To think of going through so many lives simply to arrive nowhere is not acceptable to Western minds. Belief in the New Age as a time of peace, joy, and love provides a worthwhile goal and makes reincarnation palatable to Western thinking.

Past Lives

Belief in reincarnation serves as a stimulus to belief in the New Age, because much of the current interest in New Age ideas comes from people who have, through a process called hypnotic regression, "discovered" that they have lived previously. The phenomenon of hypnosis supposedly helps them discover the nature of their past lives. Once people come to believe this, it is a short and easy step to the belief that they have come to this earth at this time for a special purpose—to bring in the New Age.

Ruth Montgomery is a good example of how this works. After she had written two books in the psychic field, her spirit guides began to give her messages about reincarnation.

Later when she came in contact with Adelle Davis, who was a leading light in the holistic health field in the 1960s, Ms. Davis introduced her to Major Arthur Knight. Knight claimed to have accidentally stumbled onto the "fact" of reincarnation by allowing a hypnotic subject to count back too far. The subject supposedly counted himself back into a previous life.

It wasn't long before Ruth Montgomery was sitting in on a hypnotic session, watching as others were "regressed" back to previous lives. At her first such session she yielded to the urge and allowed Major Knight to take her back to what she came to believe were previous lives. Imagine her surprise to find out that she had been married to her good friend Hugh Lynn Cayce, son of Edgar Cayce, millennia ago in Egypt!

Ruth's belief in the New Age is directly connected to her having come to believe in reincarnation, because once her guides had convinced her of reincarnation's validity, they could begin to feed her yet another line of argument. They have now persuaded her that numerous souls are just waiting to be here for the glorious New Age, and that some of them have come here as what she calls "walk-ins" to help with preparation for the New Age ("What Is a Walk-in?" *The New Age Catalogue*, p. 112).

Reasons for Reincarnation

From a purely logical standpoint, reincarnation is an appealing belief. At least at first glance.

It seems to bring a semblance of reason to the unreasonableness of life. It provides answers to some of life's hardest questions about justice. Why, for instance, am I sitting in a comfortable home, warm and dry despite the rain outside, while on the other side of the world more than 25 million people in Bangladesh have been driven from their homes by the worst floods in memory? Is there any justice if some are doomed to suffer every day while a privileged few live in comfort?

And if I am among the privileged few, how can I justify my lifestyle?

Reincarnation's answer to these questions is that everyone chooses his or her own place to reside before coming to this world. If a person is born on the streets of Bombay and lives the life of a crippled beggar, that should be no concern of the wealthy man who rides by in his air-conditioned car. The beggar, after all, has chosen this life of suffering to atone for something done wrong in a previous life. And the rich man is living his life of comfort because of good things done in a previous life.

It seems a simple, logical answer to a difficult question. And it certainly is effective for soothing nagging doubts about the apparent unfairness of life.

But a more careful look reveals that reincarnation does not really answer questions about justice at all. Moreover, taken to its logical conclusion, belief in reincarnation, as it is taught within the New Age movement, is one of the most convincing arguments against belief in the imminent New Age.

Logical Fallacies of Reincarnation

During the time that I was working on this manuscript and pondering reincarnation theory, three Italian Air Force jets collided in midair during an airshow at an American military base in Ramstein, West Germany. One of the jets glanced off the other two, flew up in a short arc, plummeted into a crowd of spectators, and burst into flame. More than 350 people were injured, many receiving burns serious enough to leave them maimed for life. About 50 people died—some instantly; some slowly, agonizingly. Among the dead and injured were many small children.

The explanation for this tragedy, according to New

Age reincarnation theory, is that all 350-plus people chose, before coming to this world, to suffer or die in that way. And the three pilots involved had chosen to die instantly. All of the spectators chose to go to that very airshow, and once they arrived there, they knew (not consciously, but intuitively) exactly where to stand in order to be killed or maimed, whichever they needed most for personal development. Furthermore, the bereaved relatives and friends had somehow decided that they needed just this form of sorrow in their lives to help them to grow. And the relatives who will have to spend the next several months, or perhaps the rest of their lives, caring for the maimed have chosen that as a part of the life they need to live this time around.

Such a scenario seems preposterous. The logistics involved in placing each of those souls not only in relation to the right people but in the right place at the right time would befuddle a Cray supercomputer. Yet belief in such a scenario is necessary if you accept the doctrine of reincarnation as it is being taught by New Age leaders, both spirits and humans.

A second logical fallacy in New Age reincarnation teaching concerns the implications of the current status of the people living on earth as it relates to the dawn of the New Age.

The idea behind the New Age is that enough spirits have now evolved to a sufficiently high level that they can easily make the leap into the New Age. If things are progressing so well in the spiritual evolution field, why is it that the vast majority of human souls on earth right now are living such miserable, unenlightened lives? Why is it that the majority of souls who are choosing to incarnate on the earth plane right now are choosing to incarnate in homes in which there is hardly enough food to feed the souls already living there? Isn't that rather selfish? And is it not a sign that the majority of earth souls today have a rather negative karma to work out? How can a New Age dawn with so much negative karma around?

Reincarnation is a poor explanation for the way the world is. And it doesn't really provide adequate answers to questions about justice in life.

The Bible's explanation is better. It says that although we may suffer injustice in this life, the sufferings of this present time will seem minor in comparison to eternal life. And instead of making us feel that we deserve to be privileged, the gospel calls us to help those who are suffering injustice.

Past Lives—Another Explanation

While reincarnation may not provide good answers for the big questions about justice in life, it certainly does seem to provide a logical explanation for people's apparent ability to remember past lives, doesn't it?

Perhaps. But there are other equally good explanations.

Past life regressions are done with the aid of hypnosis. While the popular view of hypnosis is that it is an infallible aid to the recovery of lost memories, such is not the case. Dr. Bernard Diamond, a professor of law and clinical psychiatry, is an authority on hypnosis. An article in the *California Law Review* contained his responses to questions on the subject. One of the most significant answers concerned the relationship between fact and fantasy in hypnotically-enhanced memory. Dr. Diamond stated that "no one, regardless of experience, can verify the accuracy of the hypnotically enhanced memory" (March 1980, pp. 333-337).

So the first possible explanation for apparent regressions to past lives is that they are merely fantasy. This seems a fairly logical explanation, especially in light of some of the details that come up in such regressions. Linda Tischler, reviewing the book *Many Masters*, written by psychiatrist Brian Weiss about one of his patients whom he accidentally regressed back to her life in ancient Egypt, comments that the patient "described a hot, sandy valley, identified herself as 'Aronda,' and said the year was 1863 B.C. (Weiss did not say how she knew the date)." Tischler's little parenthesis was intended as a jab at the idea of regression. And rightly so. How would one know which year B.C. one was living in? The B.C. numbering system was not initiated until more than 2,000 years after "Aronda's" purported life!

A second possible explanation is found in a little-known phenomenon called cryptomnesia—hidden memory.

Hidden memories are memories a person has of things done in this life, but long ago forgotten. Such hidden memories can even be developed from what one reads or thinks about. Studies have revealed that people who thought they were remembering past lives may actually have been going back to hidden memories of things read or imagined. In some cases, with further probing under hypnosis, the subject who is supposedly remembering past actions can go so far as to recall the book and even the page number on which he or she read about the events now being recalled as part of the person's own past.

One of the strongest New Age proponents of reincarnation today is Dick Sutphen. He seems an especially likely candidate for the cryptomnesia explanation because he believes himself to be the reincarnation of an outlaw who lived in the old West of the United States. Significantly, as a boy he spent all his spare time reading novels about the old West. The things he now "recalls" from a past life are no doubt hidden memories of things he read as a boy.

A third possible explanation for memories that seem to be from previous lives is direct intervention by deceptive spirits to place ideas within a mind left vacant by a hypnotic trance. If deceptive angels can speak to people who have gone into a trance through meditation, they can also place thoughts in the minds of people in a hypnotic trance. "The reader should not be confused by the supposed differences between hypnosis, Zen, Yoga, and other Eastern healing methodologies," write two leading experts on hypnosis. "Although the ritual for each differs, they are fundamentally the same" (William Kroger and William Fezler, *Hypnosis and Behavior Modification: Imagery Conditioning*, p. 412).

This seems the most logical explanation for one of the regressions Ruth Montgomery experienced. She came out of the hypnotic trance thoroughly convinced that she had once been a sister of the Lazarus mentioned in the Bible. But the Bible mentions only two sisters of Lazarus, and in her regression Ruth "saw" both Mary and Martha, so she knew she wasn't one of them. Consequently, she dismissed that particular memory as fantasy. Then a short while later a man she had never met wrote to her saying that he had "psychically received an impression that she had been a sister of Lazarus. 'It can't be true,' Ruth argued to herself, 'because I clearly saw Martha and Mary in Lazarus' living room' " (Montgomery with Garland, *Ruth Montgomery: Herald of the New Age*, p. 130).

But not long after receiving the letter, Ruth read in

a book entitled *The Aquarian Gospel of Jesus the Christ* that Lazarus indeed had had three sisters. And the third one's name had been Ruth! (*ibid.*). That the *Aquarian Gospel* purports to have been transcribed from the "akashic records" by a man in a deep meditative state ties the whole story together, illustrating that something beyond Ruth's own fantasies was at work here to bring a similar message through three independent psychic sources.

We should certainly not be surprised to find Lucifer intervening to persuade people of the doctrine of reincarnation. It is just a continuation of his old lie "You will not surely die" (Genesis 3:4, NIV).

And he seems to get fiendish glee out of playing this theme to the hilt. In almost every account I find of people recalling their past lives, one of their "pasts" involved a life of crime. The message that comes across loud and clear is that it doesn't matter what sort of life you live—you will go on to live and enjoy life again.

The Best of Both Worlds?

On the surface, New Age philosophers have apparently developed a belief system that allows them the best of both worlds. They have stripped the Eastern concept of reincarnation of its hopelessness and grafted in a heaven-like hope to replace it. Their reincarnation doctrine seems to be one of their most successful ventures at melding Eastern and Western ideas.

But the question is Will their grafted tree bear good fruit?

What the New Age hope has become is a new religion, complete with an eschatology based on little more than wishful thinking. The other major religions of the world at least have a history by which we can judge them. The New Age religion has just put forth its first spring blossoms. Dare we stake our hopes for future life on its uncertain fruits?

A Better World Yet

The newly minted New Age religion holds out its promise of a bright future based on continued refinement of the human spirit. On the other hand, the Bible record, which has stood the test of the millennia, holds out an even better hope. This better hope is based on a more realistic vision of the human spirit.

Rather than basing hope on the supposed improvement of human beings, the Bible tells us that despite our continued failings; despite the fact that you and I, left to ourselves, go from bad to worse instead of from good to better; despite the increasing weight of woe (bad karma) in our world, Someone understands our plight and can do something about it.

That Someone is God, who ministers His grace to us, not on the basis of how we have lived in our past lives, nor even on how we have lived so far in this life, but on the basis of His decision to love us in spite of our unworthiness. God does not require us to keep coming back in life after life to atone for our past.

"But because of his great love for us, God, who is rich in mercy, made us alive with Christ even when we were dead in transgressions—it is by grace you have been saved. And God raised us up with Christ and seated us with him in the heavenly realms in Christ Jesus, in order that in the coming ages he might show the incomparable riches of his grace" (Ephesians 2:4-7, NIV).

The promise of Christianity is not multiple future lives of frustration to be lived in growing closer by degrees to human perfection, but *a* future life lived in perfect union with God, whose perfection exceeds anything we can even imagine. And He is perfectly capable of making us perfect as we trust in Him.

We need not look forward to an endless series of future lives lived in less-than-perfect surroundings, but we can look forward to "a new heaven and a new earth, the home of righteousness" (2 Peter 3:13, NIV).

We need not anticipate having to decide 100 or 1,000 more times just what kind of body to live in and just how much suffering we need to go through on the way to our next death. But we can look forward to dwelling in a land where God "will wipe every tear from [our] eyes. There will be no more death or mourning or crying or pain, for the old order of things has passed away" (Revelation 21:4, NIV).

And there's one more consideration to make in examining the conflicting hopes offered by New Age religion and Christianity. Perhaps it's a little too pragmatic or even self-centered way of looking at it. But from a practical standpoint it seems worth considering. If I accept the New Age doctrine of reincarnation and place all my hopes in its humanistic solutions instead of in God, I'm putting a lot at risk if I'm wrong. Because if I'm wrong and if only those who learn to trust in God live eternally, then belief in reincarnation will get me nowhere.

If, on the other hand, I accept the Christian message of eternal life and place my trust in God for salvation, and if I live a Christian life, I can reap all the benefits of Christianity's better hope. And I can still participate fully in making this world a better place. Then if I am wrong and reincarnation is the only real hope, what have I lost? The New Age doctrine promises me reincarnation anyway, so I'll get another go-round at it!

As for me, I would rather put my trust in the Lord and the truths He has given in the Bible, which has survived for millennia longer, than in the new and untested New Age hope.

11

A Prophetic Perspective

My search for the New Age movement has taken me down highways, lanes, and even a few back alleys. I have had an opportunity to search out the movement on both coasts and in the heartland of America. Along the way I have encountered people from many walks of life who are looking for hope—looking for something better than a materialistic society can offer.

Among people with the New Age hope, I have yet to encounter one who was rude or arrogant toward me simply because I was a Christian. The closest I have come to that was when I was conducting a seminar about the New Age movement in a church. One lady, who I believe came from a New Age background, rose to her feet and stomped loudly out of the room as soon as I began to deal with biblical material.

Perhaps in the past she had encountered a bad experience in dealing with Christians, and her display of disgust was a defense against being hurt again.

Most of the people involved in the New Age

movement see no conflict between their new belief system and any established religion. They have bought in to the myth that the new beliefs preserve the best from each of the great historic religions without contradicting any important doctrines.

Some New Age leaders do have a penchant against Christianity and do everything they can to combat it. I have read, for example, that Dick Sutphen is waging a "war on fundamentalism," and this may be the case. Sutphen certainly is at the forefront of the visible New Age movement. The index to *The New Age Catalogue* contains more references to him than to any other individual or topic. And some of the statements attributed to him do have a definite anti-Christian tone. But since he puts very little in writing, preferring to sell cassette tapes of what he says, and since he is an expert at placing subliminal messages on his tapes, I have avoided listening to him. While subliminals are not as powerful as some people think, I have a healthy respect for anything that is able to influence my subconscious mind without my being able to give it rational consideration.

Speaking at a seminar I attended, Art Lindsley, of the C. S. Lewis Institute in Washington, D.C., told of a meeting between himself, other Christian leaders, and a number of New Age leaders. He felt that the dialogue had been very positive for the most part, but one of the things that impressed him most was the stories the New Age leaders told about their mistreatment at the hands of Christians.

What a sad testimony! Jesus challenges us—even commands us—not to hate or harm even those who have openly declared themselves to be against us. Jesus challenges us to love our enemies and pray for those who persecute us (Matthew 5:44).

Rather than spending our time sleuthing out evidences to prove that New Age people are out to get us, we ought to be out to win them with love. We ought to demonstrate to them that Jesus Christ has empowered us to love even those who do not agree with us!

We can, if we are truly spiritual seekers ourselves, reach out to New Age-oriented people, because our spiritual hunger gives us much in common. We can reach out to them with forgiveness for their past, grace for today, and hope for the future. Seventh-day Adventist Christians in particular have much in common with many New Age-oriented people because of our shared interest in natural ways to good health. And if they are looking for good counsel from good spirits, certainly the writings of Ellen White should interest them. Why should the somnolent sayings of a psychic healer like Edgar Cayce be getting so much attention today when Ellen White's counsels on healthful living and natural remedies are better founded, easier to read, and validated by recent research?

Reaching Out

There are many ways that we can reach out to people who are searching. We must be wise, though, for they may not be willing to immediately accept all the doctrines and dogmas that we consider part of Christianity. First and most important is to lead them to an acceptance of God and His grace. Once they have come to know God, they can gradually come to trust that His laws are not burdensome or arbitrary, but that they have been established for the good of mankind. And they can learn that God's grace provides power to live according to His will as well as forgiveness for the past.

There is now an open window of opportunity to

reach out to people who are seeking a spiritual experience. The window will not stay open long, though, for Satan and his legions of deceptive spirits are working with limitless energy and utmost intensity to garner as many into his camp as possible. Once a person has fallen prey to the deceptions of a channel or an inner guide, it becomes a thousand times harder to lead him or her away from the pleasing lies to search for further truth. And the spirit guides will do everything in their power to prevent their subjects from turning to God and the Bible.

There is a time of warfare ahead of us. A time when we will have to do battle with people inspired by Satan with hatred for Christians. But the time is not yet. Now is the time for reaching out and rescuing people. Before they fall into Satan's grasp. Before they become a part of the throng described in Revelation as answering the call of Satan, bowing to the image of the beast, and going to war against all who remain true to God.

The New Age and the Time of Trouble

The picture in Revelation 12-16 is clear.

The time is coming when Christians will have much to fear from those who have been deceived and led captive by Satan.

And at that time people who have been ensnared by the enticing doctrines and seducing spirits of the New Age will be in the forefront of those who persecute the remnant of those who trust in God.

Revelation 12 is the beginning of the warning message about what will happen at the end of time. Revelation 13 gives, in prophetic symbolism, a picture of the type of challenge to their faith that Christians will have to face if they are to receive the seal of God rather than the mark of the beast. Revelation 14 is a composite picture of the results of the choices people make between the mark and the seal. Revelation 15 gives one additional fleeting glimpse at God's protection of those who trust Him. Then follows a description of the seven horrible plagues that will fall upon all who have joined Lucifer and persisted in rebellion against God.

Revelation 12 paints a word picture that represents the conflict that has been going on in our universe ever since Lucifer first rebelled against God. The first scene portrays a pure woman—representing God's people—about to give birth to a child. Standing in front of her is a dragon, waiting to devour her offspring. This symbol represents the enmity of Lucifer (Satan) against the human race.

The picture is reminiscent of what happened in the Garden of Eden. Eve was confronted by a serpent speaking the words of Lucifer. Lucifer wanted to devour her descendants by taking control of the world and inspiring murderous hatred in people's hearts. Soon after Adam and Eve joined his rebellion against God, their firstborn son killed the secondborn.

But the confrontation pictured in Revelation between the woman and the serpent takes place in the heavens, and the woman—because she trusts in God —is given a place to hide from the serpent for "a time, times, and half a time" (Revelation 12:14, NIV). But this makes the devil even angrier, and he roars off "to make war against the rest of her offspring—those who obey God's commandments and hold to the testimony of Jesus" (verse 17, NIV).

This is where Christians and the New Age movement come into the picture.

Historically, the time period of Satan's persecution of God's people in the wilderness is over. It took place between the years A.D. 538 and 1798—especially during the Dark Ages—and was led by an apostate church that had turned away from God and had begun to compel people to look to human priests and bishops as the source of their salvation instead of to God. The movement that promoted the persecution of true Christians at that time is similar to the New Age movement in some ways because of this insistence on salvation being accomplished by humans instead of by God, by its usurpation of God's prerogatives, and by its insistence that humans can establish their own laws and their own way to salvation different from the law and the Way revealed in the Bible.*

But we are past that time. We now live in the time when Satan has directed his full fury toward the last remnant of people who are faithful to God's law and continue to bear testimony to Jesus Christ as the Saviour of the world.

Enemies of God's Law

It is easy to see how a person who has accepted the New Age message would finally end up at enmity with people who make God's law first priority in their lives and who insist that the Jesus revealed in the Bible is the one and only Christ and Saviour of the world. This testimony rubs like sandpaper on blisters against the New Age doctrine of pluralism—that there is no one truth, no one true way to salvation, but that everyone must discover his or her own truth and path to deliverance. It irritates like nettles in saddle sores against the New Age teaching that there have been many christs and that there is no returning Redeemer, but rather that we all must come to "Christ consciousness."

Revelation 12 makes it clear that in the last days

Satan will show great enmity against those who continue to respond to God instead of to him. And we can expect that those who have learned to listen to Satan speaking through channels or through their own "higher selves" will at that time begin to receive messages telling them that Christians who tune in to God's Word instead of to a god within or a spirit manifestation are standing in the way of the fulfillment of the New Age hope.

Revelation 13 pictures how this will come about. It does not involve New Age people exclusively. Nevertheless, people who have been led astray by deceptive spirits will play an important role in the final persecution of Christians who remain true to God. They will be joined in their persecuting activities by others who may have never even heard of the New Age movement, but who have been led away from God by other religions—some of them purporting to be Christian but following in the footsteps of the apostate church that was referred to in chapter 12. This apostate church is represented in chapter 13 by a beast that rises out of the sea, receives power from Satan, and then miraculously recovers from a deadly wound.

Revelation 13 makes it plain that all those who have not learned to trust totally in God as He has revealed Himself throughout history in the Bible will join in persecuting those who remain true to God. It matters not whether they are part of an apostate Christian church, part of another Western religion, or whether they have no religion. It matters not whether they accept the New Age religion of making themselves gods, or are part of an Eastern religion that does the same. If they haven't learned to trust the God who reveals Himself in the Bible, they will be led astray and will end up persecuting those who do trust God.

A PROPHETIC PERSPECTIVE

Here's how it will come about, according to Revelation 13:11-18.

A civil government (represented by Revelation's symbol for nations, a beast) that came on the scene of history just at the time when the persecution of A.D. 538 to 1798 was ending will appear at first to be Christian in nature: "He had two horns like a lamb." (Throughout Revelation the lamb symbolizes Christ.) But the message of this lamblike nation will be like that of the old serpent Satan—"But he spoke like a dragon" (verse 11, NIV).

Speaking for Satan, this government will deceive and lead astray all people who do not follow God. In this work it will be aided, according to Revelation 16:13-16, by deceptive spirits who will help unite all nations in their enmity against God and His people.

Remember, deceptive messages are already being delivered to people worldwide by the agency of channels, psychics, spirit guides, and even computers! This is part of the New Age movement, but it is not only New Age people who are receiving the messages.

The lamblike beast will work miracles (courtesy of Satan's power) to impress people, even "causing fire to come down from heaven to earth in full view of men" (verse 13, NIV). Some Bible students suggest that this is a sort of false Pentecost, because on the Day of Pentecost tongues of fire came down from God and rested on the assembled Christians. A false Pentecost would involve the gift of the deceptive spirits being given to Satan's followers. This may be what is happening right now with the burgeoning number of channels and their followers.

UFO expert Brad Steiger, in a book about the large number of people who have begun to receive messages from purported extraterrestrial UFOnauts, reported that the spirits speaking to one channel had indicated that "from this brief visual encounter with an unidentified object in the sky came another linkup in a new Pentecost which would offer revelations for the dawning age of Aquarius. On this occasion cosmic 'tongues of flame' had somehow reached out of the mysterious craft to dance about the attractive head of Robin McPherson" (*The Aquarian Revelations*, p. 10). Robin began to receive many messages—the most important of which proved to be deceptive.

No one nation is currently lending its authority to this false Pentecost, but according to this prophecy, this may soon come about.

The Image to the Beast

Next, the lamblike beast will erect what is termed an "image to the beast" and seek to compel people to worship it. This image harks back to the story of Daniel 3, which tells of three Hebrew men who had the courage, despite a death threat, to refuse to bow down to an image that the Babylonian king Nebuchadnezzar had erected to represent his eternal rule over all the earth.

Revelation 13's image to the beast represents the continuing authority of the power that persecuted Christians during the Dark Ages. Bowing down to this image will involve disloyalty to the law of God and swearing fealty to the manmade law that this apostate power has substituted for the law of God. Bowing down will also signify acceptance of this power's claim that its rebellion against God can go on for eternity. And the lamblike beast demands that everyone bow down to this symbol of Lucifer's rebellion against God on pain of death.

Those who capitulate to this pressure receive the

mark of the beast in their foreheads or hands. They also receive the number of its name—666.

As we saw in chapter 7, this number represents mankind's incompleteness apart from God. It represents human beings' attempts to save themselves through hopes such as that which the New Age provides. There is also a special significance to it in relation to the beast from the sea, whose mark it is.

Six or Seven

Remember that human beings were created on the *sixth* day of Creation week. They were complete and perfect only as long as they maintained contact with God. God provided the *seventh* day of the week as the rest day—the Sabbath—when Adam and Eve and all their offspring were to take time off from their human-centered, self-preservation activities and spend time in special contact with their Creator. God rested that day, not because He was tired, but because He wanted to enjoy the fruits of His creation. He wanted to enjoy walking and talking with Adam and Eve. Thus the number 7, the seventh-day Sabbath, represented the time for Adam and Eve to be perfected through contact with and trust in God.

Later, when God gave the Ten Commandments to mankind, He placed a reminder of that rest day right at the heart of the ten. "Remember the Sabbath day by keeping it holy," He wrote in stone. "Six days you shall labor and do all your work, but the seventh day is a Sabbath to the Lord your God. On it you shall not do any work, neither you, nor your son or daughter. . . . For in six days the Lord made the heavens and the earth, the sea, and all that is in them, but he rested on the seventh day. Therefore the Lord blessed the Sabbath day and made it holy" (Exodus 20:8-11, NIV).

By giving this reminder in the midst of the law He wrote on stone, God made it plain that He wanted His people to keep the seventh day as a special time for remembering His creative power and worshiping Him forever.

A few chapters later in Exodus God explained that He wants His people to keep the Sabbath as a special sign that He is the one who sanctifies, or makes them holy (Exodus 31:13). And centuries later the prophet Isaiah pointed to the holy Sabbath hours as the time when God's people would learn to find their delight in the Lord whom they would worship throughout eternity (see Isaiah 58:13, 14).

The Sabbath, then, is a key fixture in God's plan to bring about a better world—the new earth He has promised.

It is highly significant, then, that one of the chief symbols of the apostate church's rebellion against God and His law lies in its claim to have the authority to change the law of God, specifically as it relates to the seventh day of the week, the Sabbath!

The number 666 represents mankind's rebellion against God and substitution of his own way of salvation, his own law. And the image to the rebellious beast involves human laws that have obscured the seventh-day Sabbath and left people ignorant of God's contact point for perfecting them. By substituting in its place another day (Sunday, the first day of the week) for church attendance, the apostate church has left people stuck on the number 6. Most Christians treat Sunday merely as a holiday. Because there is no biblical authority for making it a rest day, they use it for their own pleasure and business pursuits instead of for coming into contact with God and receiving His perfecting influence. And they ignore Saturday, the seventh day that was set aside to bring us up to the level of 7 through contact with God.

In bowing down to this image, people will join in the rebellion against the law of God that calls them back to Him every seventh day of the week. And hence they will be left imperfect—with 666, the number of humanity, instead of the perfection that comes from contact with God on the *seven*th-day Sabbath.

Revelation 14 pictures the contrast between those who receive the mark of the beast by rebelling against God and those who receive the seal of God by following the Lamb (the true Lamb, Jesus Christ, not the false one who speaks like a dragon) wherever He goes. These saints, who remain on God's side, are described in much the same way they were in Revelation 12. Their distinguishing characteristics are that they "obey God's commandments and remain faithful to Jesus" (Revelation 14:12, NIV).

They have staked their lives on faith and obedience, for in Revelation 13 the lamblike beast issues a death decree against all who refuse to bow down to the image representing rebellion against God.

They maintain their faith in God, for one of the decrees against those who refuse to bow to the image in chapter 13 is that they will be refused the right to buy and sell. In other words, they will have to depend fully on God to provide their needs, rather than on business transactions with other human beings.

In this dependence on God they become perfected. This perfection comes not through living multiple lives to work out the flaws in their characters, but through contact with the divine, perfecting power God gives to those who will come to Him and spend the time with Him that He has set aside for bringing humans up to the level of 7.

By spending daily and weekly time with God, abandoning their self-centered pursuits to maintain their contact with God on His Sabbath day, these people have been prepared for the time when they have to abandon trust in human pursuits for sustenance. And by spending time with Him in their life on this earth, they have prepared themselves to enjoy eternity with God in the new earth. This is one of the promised results of keeping the Sabbath holy, according to Isaiah 58:13, 14.

Hope for Everyone

The new earth hope is available to everyone, not just to the elite who are ready for a higher stage of evolution.

It is available to you. You can inherit this hope by beginning to trust God fully with your life. Then begin to study His revelations recorded in the Bible. Don't be discouraged when you see the high goals God has for you. He can empower you to reach them.

Don't be captivated by seductive spirits who have come here to deceive. The hope they hold out is really only a hoax. Trust God and learn to obey Him, and you will be among those who inherit the land without tears, pain, or death.

---

*It is not the intent of this book to discuss the details of this already fulfilled prophecy. For a thorough discussion of this phase of the prophecy, which occurs in a slightly different form in the Old Testament book of Daniel, see C. Mervyn Maxwell, *God Cares*, vol. 1, pp. 116-141. The book is published by Pacific Press Publishing Association, Box 7000, Boise, Idaho 83707. Pacific Press books may be ordered by telephone with a major credit card. Call (800) 447-7377 within the United States.

Bibliography

Alexander, Brooks. "Theology From the Twilight Zone." *Christianity Today*, Sept. 18, 1987, p. 26.

Bach, Richard. *Jonathan Livingston Seagull*. New York: The Macmillan Co., 1970.

Belostock, Jane. "Demystifying New Age Books." *Publishers Weekly*, June 24, 1988, pp. 58, 60.

Blodgett, Ralph. "Can Psychics and Astrologers Predict the Future?" *Vibrant Life*, July/August 1986, pp. 14-19.

The New Age Catalogue, New York: Doubleday, 1988.

Brooke, Anthony. *Revelation for the New Age*. London: Regency Press, 1967.

Campbell, Joseph. *The Way of the Animal Powers*. London: Summerfield Press, 1983. Vol. 1.

Capra, Fritjof. *The Tao of Physics*. Rev. ed. New York: Bantam Books, 1984.

_____. *The Turning Point*. New York: Bantam Books, 1983.

Carter, Mary Ellen. *Edgar Cayce on Prophecy*. New York: Warner Books, 1968.

"Christ, The." *New Teachings for an Awakening Humanity*. Santa Clara, Calif.: Spiritual Endeavors Pub. Co., 1986.

Cumbey, Constance. *The Hidden Dangers of the Rainbow*. Shreveport, La.: Huntington House, 1983.

Dass, Ram. *Grist for the Mill*. New York: Bantam, 1979.

De Chardin, Pierre Teilhard. *How I Believe*. Rene Hague, tr. New York: Harper and Row, 1969.

Diamond, Bernard L. "Inherent Problems in the Use of Pretrial Hypnosis on a Prospective Witness," *California Law Review*, March 1980, pp. 333-337.

Essene, Virginia, ed. *New Teachings for an Awakening Humanity*. Santa Clara, Calif.: SEE Pub. Co., 1986.

Ferguson, Marilyn. *The Aquarian Conspiracy*. Los Angeles: J. P. Tarcher, Inc., 1980.

Findhorn Community, The. *The Findhorn Garden*. New York: Harper and Row, 1975.

Ford, Arthur. *Unknown but Known*. New York: Signet Mystic Book, 1968.

Geisler, Norman L., and J. Yutaka Amano. *The Reincarnation Sensation*. Wheaton, Ill.: Tyndale House Publishers, Inc., 1986.

Hackett, Alice Payne, and James Henry Burke. *80 Years of Best-Sellers*. New York: R. R. Bowker, 1977.

Hexham, Irving, and Karla Poewe. *Understanding Cults and New Religions*. Grand Rapids: Wm. B. Eerdmans, 1986.

Hubbard, Barbara Marx. *Happy Birthday Planet Earth*. Santa Fe, N. Mex.: Ocean Tree Books, 1986.

Hunt, Dave, and T. A. McMahon. *The Seduction of Christianity*. Eugene, Oreg. Harvest House, 1985.

Keel, John A. *UFOs—Operation Trojan Horse*. New York: G. P. Putnam's Sons, 1970.

Kroger, William, and William Fezler. *Hypnosis and Behavior Modification: Imagery Conditioning*. New York: Lippincott, 1976.

"Lazaris on 1987." *New Realities*, July/August 1987, p. 29.

Lister, Johnny. *The New Age*. San Francisco: Entheos, 1984.

Marrs, Texe. *Dark Secrets of the New Age*. Westchester, Ill.: Crossway Books, 1987.

_____ *Mystery Mark of the New Age*. Westchester, Ill.: Crossway Books, 1988.

Martin, Katherine. "The Voice of Lazaris." *New Realities*, July/August 1987, p. 28.

McLaughlin, Corrinne. "Tuning In to the Best Channel." *New Realities*, July/August 1987, p. 38.

Miller, Elliot. "Channeling—Spiritistic Revelations for

the New Age." *Christian Research Journal*, Winter/Spring 1988, p. 17.

Mitchell, Edgar D. "Introduction: From Outer Space to Inner Space." In John White, ed. *Psychic Exploration*. New York: G. P. Putnam's Sons, 1974.

Montgomery, Ruth. *A Gift of Prophecy*. New York: Bantam Books, 1966.

_____ *Aliens Among Us*. New York: Putnam Publishing Group, 1985.

_____ *Threshold to Tomorrow*. New York: G. P. Putnam's Sons, 1982.

_____ "What Is a Walk-in?" *The New Age Catalogue*, p. 112.

_____ with Joanne Garland. *Ruth Montgomery: Herald of the New Age*. New York: Ballantine, 1986.

New Age Catalogue, The. New York: Doubleday, 1988.

"New Age Harmonies," *Time*, Dec. 7, 1987, p. 62.

Popenoe, Oliver and Cris. *Seeds of Tomorrow—New Age Communities That Work*. San Francisco: Harper and Row, 1984.

Psychic Journeys. Alexandria, Va.: Time-Life Books, 1987.

Pyramid Books and the New-Age Collection Catalog. Salem, Mass.: Pyramid Books, undated but from 1988.

Ramtha. Cohn, Richard, ed. *I Am Ramtha*. Portland, Oreg.: Beyond Words, Publishing, 1986.

_____ with Douglas James Mahr. *Voyage to the New World*. New York: Fawcett, 1985.

Raphaell, Katrina. *Crystal Healing, Vol. 2—The Therapeutic Application of Crystals and Stones*. Santa Fe, N. Mex.: Aurora Press, 1987.

Rayl, A.J.S. "UFO Poll." *Omni*, October 1987, p. 144.

Reisser, Paul C., Teri K. Reisser, and John Weldon.

New Age Medicine. Downers Grove, Ill.: InterVarsity Press, 1987.

Roberts, Jane. *The Seth Material*. New York: Prentice Hall, 1987.

Rogers, Spencer L. *The Shaman*. Springfield, Ill.: Charles C. Thomas, 1982.

Ross, Nancy Wilson. *Three Ways of Asian Wisdom*. New York: Simon and Schuster, 1966.

Roszak, Theodore. *The Making of a Counter Culture*. New York: Doubleday and Co., 1969.

_____ *Unfinished Animal*. New York: Harper and Row, 1975.

Rudhyar, Dane. *The Astrology of America's Destiny*. New York: Random House, 1974.

_____ *Occult Preparations for a New Age*. Wheaton, Ill.: Theosophical Publishing House, 1975.

Smith, Lynn. "The New, Chic Metaphysical Fad of Channeling." *Los Angeles Times*, Dec. 5, 1986.

Spangler, David. *Revelation: The Birth of a New Age*. Elgin, Ill.: Lorian Press, 1976.

Steiger, Brad, ed., *The Aquarian Revelations*. New York: Dell, 1971.

Thompson, William Irwin. *Passages About Earth*. New York: Harper and Row, 1973.

Watring, Richard. "New Age Training in Business: Mind Control in Upper Management?" *Eternity*, February 1988, p. 30.

White, John. "A Course in Miracles: Spiritual Wisdom for the New Age." *Science of Mind*, March 1986, pp. 10-14, 80-88.

Young, Meredith Lady. *Agartha*. Walpole, N.H.: Stillpoint Publishing, 1984.